MUSCLE BUILDING FOR BEGINNERS

MUSCLE BUILDING FOR BEGINNERS

By

MICHAEL FALLON

AND

JIM SAUNDERS

Mr. Universe, Class II

AN ARC BOOK

ARCO PUBLISHING COMPANY, INC.

219 Park Avenue South, New York, N.Y. 10003

All photographs in this book, not otherwise
credited, are by Vince Studio and Camera-
craft. Line drawings for Part I by Jak, and
for Part II by Ben.

The publishers wish to acknowledge the
assistance of Jon Twitchell and the Weider
Barbell Co., in obtaining several invaluable
photographs for this book.

Eleventh Printing, 1977

An ARC Book
Published by Arco Publishing Company, Inc.
219 Park Avenue South, New York, N.Y. 10003

Library of Congress Catalog Card Number 64-10506
ISBN 0-668-01131-9

Printed in the United States of America

CONTENTS

PART I

by MICHAEL FALLON

PART II

by JIM SAUNDERS

Part I

by

MICHAEL FALLON

CHAPTER I

WHY EXERCISE?

Why exercise?

Well, there are almost as many answers to that as there are ways of exercising. Some people exercise to grow strong, some to get big muscles, some to make themselves fit and well.

Take my own case, for example, and I mention it merely because I believe it can inspire people who, like me, have no particular aptitude for exercise and at first have no idea of ever doing any.

Halfway through the war I was wounded, blown up, and my lungs torn and damaged. Doctors, plenty of them, gave me two years to live at the most and told me that from that time on I was to take things gently: not to exert myself too much, for fear of bringing things to a head.

And for a year I followed their advice, never standing when I could sit, never sitting when I could lie down, never moving when I could lie still. It made me no stronger: in fact I got weaker and weaker and sicker and sicker. I weighed no more than 85 pounds and could hardly walk across the road without making myself ill.

Yet today I consider that injury the most wonderful thing that ever happened to me, because it transformed my life to become eventually more full and more happy than it had ever been before. For it was then that I discovered the value of physical exercise.

Up to that time I had been a journalist. My life had been sedentary, even before the war, and I had never played games or taken part in sport, so I can honestly say that I had no previous athletic background to help me on. In fact, I was very much like thousands of other men, except that I was probably much weaker.

My chest at no time measured more than thirty-two

inches round, and when I bought my first barbell set a
year after the doctors had given me up, it was all I could
do to lift the empty bar above my head. My first exercises
were performed with an empty dumb-bell bar, weighing
no more than five pounds, in each hand.

Yet today, over fifteen years later, I weigh 185 pounds,
can press two hundred pounds, and regularly perform
ten repetitions in the squat with more than three hundred
pounds on my shoulders. And I hold an insurance policy
with a well-known firm as a first-class life!

As I progressed I studied more and more carefully
the science of physical culture. I collected a library of
books about me: I visited nearly every strong man in the
country at his home or his gym: as a journalist I inter-
viewed thousands of professional wrestlers, weight-lifters,
strand-pullers, athletes, and discussed with them their
training methods, and I have written many millions of
words on what I found out.

And what I found out surprised me.

In many cases these strong men and body-builders
had started off from an extremely weak physical structure.
They were not all born strong but they made themselves
strong by hard work and the application of scientific
principles to their exercising.

Some of them, as professionals, spent many hours a
day over their work-outs and naturally they found a high
degree of success. But there is no real need for long exercise
periods, provided you increase the amount of weight you use
to the point where the heaviness of the work-out compen-
sates for its shortness.

As shown in a later chapter, hundreds of deep knee
bends with no weight on the shoulders are needed to
produce the same effect as ten or twenty squats with a
barbell weighing, say, two hundred pounds.

Naturally, you will not be able to start using a two
hundred pound barbell in your first exercise period, but
by exercising consistently with a weight that is within your
strength limit and adding to its poundage regularly as
advocated in the schedule of repetitions, in little over a
year you will be squatting with two hundred pounds, and

Jimmy Stevens displays the physique that won
him the coveted title of Junior Mr. Britain

Mervynne Cotter displays a physique that is both tough and muscular

in the other exercises you will be using weights that would amaze you now.

This is not to say that the weights you use will continue to increase easily and regularly every month. No one can forecast now exactly what poundages you will be able to use in twelve months' time, and there will be 'sticking points' when it will be impossible for you to add a single ounce more to the bar, even though the schedule may call for the weight to be increased.

The only thing to do at such times is to persevere, to 'keep on keeping on', and eventually you will find yourself passing that point. You will find yourself growing huskier, your muscles becoming bigger and stronger, your strength doubling and trebling itself.

Even the fact that you work at a hard and tiring job during the day is no bar to regular exercise during the evening. Three hours a week, one hour per exercise period on alternate evenings, will be sufficient to bring results such as you may never have dreamed of. And at the same time you will build a new strength and vigour that will enable you to go through your day's work more easily, leaving plenty over for your evening's work-out.

A man who built himself what was perhaps one of the finest physiques the world has ever seen, John C. Grimek, did it while working long hours at a manual job. And side by side with his matchless muscles, he developed a strength that turned him into a weight-lifting champion.

Nor do you need expensive apparatus. Many a man has started on the road to a better physique with nothing more to help him than the everyday things that can be found around the house.

Edward Aston, for instance, who eventually became 'Britain's Strongest Man', performed his first work-outs with a broom-handle on which he hung paint cans filled with stones. And this improvised barbell enabled him to perform most of the standard exercises and to increase the poundage by adding more stones as needed.

Look around you. Perhaps in your house there are a couple of old flat-irons. What better substitutes could be found for a pair of dumb-bells? And how about a couple of buckets filled with mould from the garden, heavy books, a sack of sand or earth with the mouth tightly tied, a couple of big stones?

If you will but follow the courses outlined in this book, never missing an exercise period, and conscientiously putting your best efforts into every movement, success will be yours, despite every difficulty.

CHAPTER II

RESULTS YOU MAY EXPECT

How much? How long? These are the two questions that every physical training instructor gets hurled at him more than any other. And no two questions, let us be honest, are more difficult to answer.

No one but a charlatan will take an untrained man and by looking at his measurements tell him what his measurements are likely to be in six or twelve months' time, or even what his ultimate measurements are likely to be. And when they do attempt it, they are always wrong, as far as my experience goes, anyway.

So much depends on a man's potentialities, and I defy anyone to forecast those entirely accurately from his measurements. And a great deal more depends on the way he takes to the work, how much he sticks at it, and the amount of effort he puts into it.

Men who have been diagnosed by the 'experts' as too light boned to make very quick progress have by their application to the exercises and 'stick-at-ability' confounded all predictions and become outstanding in a short while. Others, said to have a great future before them, have taken it easy when training and have been slower to respond.

But there is one thing that is always encouraging to remember: this is a game in which there are no failures. Follow the exercises faithfully for four weeks, and at the end of that time you will be fitter, stronger, more muscular than you are today. *How much* more muscular depends on you and the amount of work you put into it.

Yet, despite this, I will not tell you that you can transform a weak, sickly body into a mountain of muscle in that time, and you would not expect me to. Nor will I tell you that you can do it in six months, though in six months I have known men in their teens and early twenties to make truly remarkable improvements in their health and strength —so much so that they were almost unrecognizable as the same men they had been those few short months before.

I have seen fat men knock a waist-line down from forty inches to thirty in that length of time, almost half an inch a week, and at the same time become fitter and more muscular than they ever were before. I've seen pale, pimply, undersized youths add 30 pounds or more to their weight and a couple of inches in height, and without the use of built-up shoes, either.

But if you pin me down to hard promises, I will make one. With my hand on my heart I will tell you that if you have never exercised before, in one week you will feel the difference, will know that something tremendous is happening to you.

In one month you will not only feel the difference, but will be able to *see* it. Your muscles will have become hard and firm. You will no longer become breathless when you run for a bus. Your posture will have improved and you will be tingling with new life. And what is more, people will be beginning to comment on your new appearance, the healthy glow in your cheeks, the sparkle in your eye.

After the three months' resistance exercises you will, if you are underweight, be anything up to 15 lbs. heavier, with square shoulders, a chest that is fast growing into a power-house, legs that are filled with a new spring and vigour. Or if you are now fat and overweight, you will have taken off a similar amount of dead flab and be sprouting with new muscle, and you will have found a seemingly unlimited supply of energy and 'go' that will surprise you and leave your friends gasping.

But the benefits of regular training do not end there.

In a year you may expect to have doubled your strength, to be pressing about 130 lb. and to be cleaning and jerking about 170 lb. In a year you may expect to be raising about 300 lb. in the dead-lift, that fundamental test of a man's power. And remember that, in a year, men have risen from obscurity to become prize-winning figures in national physique contests.

CHAPTER III

THE APPARATUS NEEDED

WITH free exercise you can achieve wonders with your health and appearance, with improvised weights even more, but eventually the time will come when you will want to consider buying some equipment. What sort of equipment will you buy?

The magazines are filled with advertisements of what can perhaps best be described as 'trick' apparatus: various complicated spring mechanisms and unusual devices. These are no doubt all very good in their way, and each has something to offer that is peculiarly its own, but they are for the man who already has the standard équipment and feels justified in investing in something to 'tinker' with.

The novice just starting in body-building cannot do better than obtain an ordinary disc-loading barbell, consisting of a steel bar one inch in diameter, and an ample supply of flat discs. Among these should be plenty of small discs of the $1\frac{1}{4}$-lb. and $2\frac{1}{2}$-lb. variety, for it is these that make the progression of poundages easy.

Most barbell sets nowadays include a couple of short dumb-bell rods. If yours doesn't, it is easy enough to convert it to a dumb-bell set at any time by buying a couple of rods, which can usually be obtained for a few dollars. Similarly, a dumb-bell set can be converted to a barbell set at any time, though this is usually a more expensive process as the quality of the steel bar used in a barbell set must be high, particularly with a heavy set.

If you have the room to use a barbell, I suggest this is what you buy, but you will need to be able to clear a space about eight feet square at a minimum. Follow the barbell courses as outlined, and occasionally spend a few weeks on one of the dumb-bell courses as a change and to break up the monotony of the routine. You are one of the lucky ones.

But if space is limited and there is no room to swing a barbell, there is still no need to despair. Dumb-bells are a wonderful way of building the physique. They get at the muscles from many different angles, and because of the necessity to *balance* them in the hands while performing the exercises, they are, in some ways, superior to the barbell.

Some men do not even have a bedroom to train in and, living in digs and perhaps always travelling from town to town, they get little chance to use heavy equipment. For such men cables are ideal.

Here again, don't go in for 'trick' equipment, but concentrate on buying the best chest expander of a normal type that you can obtain.

There are three types of chest expander on the market:

1. *The steel spring strand*, which is excellent for most of the exercises, but has the disadvantage that it is heavy to carry about if you do much travelling. It is also inclined to be cold to the touch, and sometimes pinches the body rather painfully in some of the movements.

2. *The solid rubber strand*, which stretches further than any other type, but because it is exposed to the open air has a tendency to crack, particularly at the ends where they are bound to the metal fastenings. And, of course, once a crack develops in a rubber strand, its days of usefulness are numbered!

3. *The rubber strand with a cotton sheath covering*. This will not stretch as far as a strand made of bare rubber, but has the advantage that it is protected from the atmosphere and therefore has a longer life. It is the most popular, and in my opinion is the best one to buy.

Later you may want to buy other equipment and there are all sorts of items that can be useful.

If you are a strand-puller there is a strand-sculling exerciser, a wall exerciser and various all-purpose exercisers with combination foot stirrups and hand-grips. In addition there are various spring exercisers that call for pressure instead of pulling, usually called 'crusher grips' and similar names. All these are good for achieving that little extra once you have laid a solid foundation of muscle on which to build.

If you are a weight-lifter, you will be attracted by incline benches, squat stands, abdominal boards, calf machines, lat machines and the like. All these have their purpose, but if you are wise you will not bother about them just at the moment.

First concentrate on the standard exercises, stick to the courses set out in the following pages, and leave specialized apparatus to the man it is intended for—the advanced barbell trainer. You will not be ready for it for at least a year.

CHAPTER IV

HOW TO TRAIN

How you will train depends on what you are hoping to achieve. If you want sheer brute strength, you will train with heavy weights and low repetitions, concentrating on a few heavy exercises performed in a long series of sets. If you want big muscles and are not particularly concerned with strength, you will perform a peculiar sort of routine of half-movements with light weights, known as 'muscle-spinning'.

But if your aim is a good physique with first-class health and muscles that are not only big but have the strength to back up their impressive appearance, that is what this book aims to give you.

The first basic courses will build you up if you are thin, and will reduce your size if you are fat. This may sound funny to the beginner: that the same exercises will do both jobs, but the secret is that a good exercise course *normalizes* the body and irons out whatever defects you have.

Take accurate measurements of yourself and record them in a notebook, because only by this means can you check up and find out how much you have improved. If you can have a photograph of yourself taken in a bathing costume, do so—it'll give you something to look back on and laugh over in a few months' time when you have earned your new physique.

In your notebook also record the exercises you follow and, when you come to the resistance courses, the amount of weight you use in them. Week by week you will be able to watch your strength grow.

Don't be tempted into any 'crank' diet, no matter what you may read in a health magazine. Eat only good wholesome food, with something of everything mentioned in the diet chart on page 20 and you won't go far wrong.

Strong tea and coffee are not good beverages for the body-builder, and milk, water and fruit juices are better. An occasional glass of beer does no harm, but don't drink to excess.

If you suffer from constipation, this must be eradicated as soon as possible, but *don't* try to cure it by means of pills. Such artificial remedies leave the constitution weak and are inclined to make the constipation even worse. Before long you become a slave to the pill-box and are unable to do without its aid.

The best cure for constipation is plain, pure water. Two pints of it, drunk slowly every day will have you 'right' in no time. There is no need to drink the water all at once—have a glass by you and sip it during the day. For a short while you may try taking water instead of tea or coffee after meals; it's a good habit and one well worth cultivating.

Do not try to work out every day with weights or strands, such a practice is too exhausting. The best results come if you exercise every other day, or seven times a fortnight. Once every two months take a clear week off, to prevent staleness and over-training.

How much weight you can use in each exercise will

naturally depend on you. The poundages given in the schedule of repetitions are intended as a guide, and you should experiment for yourself and find out what suits you. The idea is to finish the training session with a feeling of exhilaration and not in a state of exhaustion.

Sleep is most important when you are following a heavy training routine. Get at least eight hours a day, more if you can manage it, and don't try to skimp by cutting half an hour on weekdays and staying in bed till noon on Sundays. Rest can't be lent and borrowed in that way.

Exercise should be carried out in a warm, well-ventilated room, and you should wear a suspensory, a pair of bathing trunks or an old pair of flannels, and a sweater. Always keep warm and do not stand or sit in a draught between exercises.

After you have finished your routine, take a warm bath or a shower, or wash down well with a flannel and warm water. Then wrap up and allow the body to cool slowly.

Exercise should always be carried out in the evening. Do not exercise in the morning, except for the short schedule of limbering exercises for the over-weight mentioned on page 21 as at this time the sugar content and nervous energy are both low.

A word of warning. If you are very fat and you have a protruding stomach, do not attempt the 'sit-up' or 'abdominal raise' mentioned in the following courses until your stomach has been reduced a little. Nor should you attempt any form of toe-touching from a standing position.

When the stomach is already over-loaded, these exercises will tend to aggravate the condition and make it worse.

CHAPTER V

HOW TO SLIM—THE EASY WAY

MOST of the people in this world want to change their figures, or so it seems from my mail-bag. Either they're too fat and want to get thinner, or they're too thin and

Alan Harvey proves that a weight-trainer can be both
supple and agile as he balances on a pair of dumb-bells

Gerry Hayward, already in good shape and potentially a world champion.

want to get fatter. Seems there's no pleasing anyone in this world!

The first thing that occurs to a man who wants to lose weight is to diet, and basically that is the answer to the whole problem. But dieting does not mean depriving the body of food, as so many so-called experts suggest. Balanced diet is the thing to aim at, and it is up to you to make sure you are eating food of every type, fats and starches as well as green vegetables.

The body is like a bank: pay into it so many calories per day by means of eating and you will establish a 'credit'. Withdraw a certain number of calories a day by using up energy and you will 'balance the books' at the end of the day.

If you pay in more than you take out, your account will grow and you will become fat. If you take out more than you put in, your account will diminish, and you will grow thin.

There are obviously two ways of making your account smaller. You may put in less calories by eating less, or you may take out more by using up more energy—in other words, by exercise.

Don't be tempted to cut out all foods said to be 'fattening', such as fats and starches, for if you do there is every likelihood that you will make yourself ill, as serious diseases can be caused by vitamin deficiency. To give one or two examples of this, Vitamin A is present in milk, butter, cream, egg-yolk, cheese, fat meat and cod-liver oil. It promotes growth and helps to ward off infection and particularly skin diseases. Vitamin B is present in potatoes, milk, eggs and cereals, and lack of it causes nervous disorders and stomach trouble.

By cutting out the so-called 'fattening' foods you are cutting down on your supplies of those two essential vitamins.

The other way of slimming is to eat normally and to exercise regularly. This will balance the books favourably for you and yet will ensure that you get all the vitamins you need.

But of course, there is the fact that many fat people do

carry out some form of exercise. 'I walk for miles', they will tell you, 'yet it does not have the least effect on me.'

Not all exercise is equally beneficial. In fact, some forms of exercise may be positively harmful by sapping vitality while giving little positive value in return.

And exercise must get at the parts that need slimming. If your waist-line is too thick, it is the waist-line that must be exercised. If your hips and posterior bulge in all directions, you must get at these parts with your exercising.

Free exercise is good, particularly for men who are out of condition, but its results are slow in coming, and long before a really noticeable effect is achieved, the results stop altogether. The only really fast and efficient form of exercise is with added resistance in the form of weights or cables.

For the next four weeks watch your food, making sure you get some of each of the seven groups every day, and follow out the easy exercise routine given in this chapter.

GROUP 1.   Meat, poultry, fish, eggs, nuts, peas, etc.

GROUP 2.   Green vegetables: lettuce, watercress, and yellow vegetables: carrots, etc.

GROUP 3.   Fresh citrus fruit: oranges, grapefruit, etc.

GROUP 4.   Apples, pears, bananas and other fruit.

GROUP 5.   Starches: bread, flour, cereals.

GROUP 6.   Milk and milk products: cheese, etc.

GROUP 7.   Butter and other fats.

Peter Moorhouse is built on classical lines and
has extremely good abdominal definition

Tom Cameron, a young body-builder whose fine
physique has won him much acclaim

FREE EXERCISE CHART
For those who want to get slim

1. Leg Raise (20 reps).
2. Leg Spread (20 reps).
3. Leg Thrust (20 reps).
4. Side Bend (20 reps each way).
5. Trunk Twist (20 reps each way).
6. Leg Swinging (till tired).

The above short schedule of free exercises should be followed every morning in addition to the general courses recommended in the following chapters.

The exercises are performed as follows:

1. *Leg Raise.* See Chapter VIII, exercise 8, but take the movement only to the position at which the legs are at right angles to body.

2. *Leg Spread.* Lying on back, raise legs until they are at right angles to body. This is the commencing position. Open the legs, spreading them to sides as far as possible. Return to centre and repeat.

3. *Leg Thrust.* Lie on back and draw knees up to chest. Keeping heels a few inches above floor, straighten the legs vigorously.

4. *Side Bend.* See Chapter VIII, exercise 3.

5. *Trunk Twist.* See Chapter VIII, exercise 4.

6. *Leg Swinging.* Stand on toes of right foot with tips of right fingers against wall to help maintain balance. Swing left leg forward and backwards vigorously and rhythmically, keeping knee straight. Repeat till tired, then perform with right leg.

CHAPTER VI

HOW TO GAIN WEIGHT

THE problem of the thin man is, as might be expected, exactly the opposite of the fat man's problem. The thin man doesn't put enough into his bank to build up a credit balance.

In addition he may find that, although he eats more, he still doesn't put on weight. The answer lies in stimulating the metabolic processes with a few repetition exercises with really heavy weights, and cutting out all minor movements involving small muscle groups.

At the same time the intake of food and drink must be increased, and all opportunities to rest when not actually exercising must be taken.

One of the most beneficial foods of all for weight-gaining is milk, and you should try to drink two or three pints of this a day. Not all need be taken straight from the glass—make it into rice puddings, junkets, porridge, etc., or have milk drinks such as cocoa, hot chocolate, malted milk. In hot weather, milk shakes, made by mixing a small amount of squash or fruit cordial with milk and beating ice-cream into it, is most pleasant.

Try to get an extra hour's sleep each night, and if the opportunity occurs, rest a little with the feet up after meals.

Follow the free exercise course for one month, and then the resistance course of your choice for the next three months. This may do all you need in the way of packing on weight and muscle. If you want to be still bigger, proceed to one of the bulk courses as outlined in the schedule.

You will see that each schedule consists of five exercises, and these exercises should be performed in sets of three. For instance, if you are doing the free exercise schedule for weight-gaining, you will take the first exercise in the schedule, Chair Dips, and perform ten repetitions. Rest for a short while—one or two minutes is best—and then perform ten

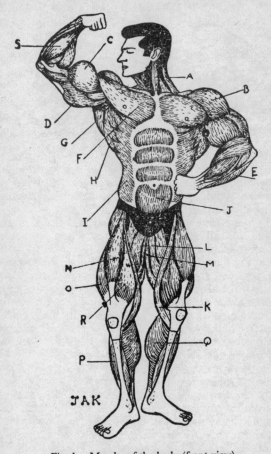

Fig. 1. Muscles of the body (front view).
A. Sterno-cleido-mastoid. B. Deltoid. C. Biceps. D. Triceps.
E. Flexor Carpi Ulnaris. F. Pectoralis Major. G. Latissimus Dorsi.
H. Serratus Magnus. I. Obliquus Externus Abdominis. J. Rectus
Abdominis. K. Sartorius. L. Adductor Longus. M. Adductor
Magnus. N. Rectus Femoris. O. Vastus Externus. P. Tibialis
Anticus. Q. Gastrocnemius. R. Vastus Internus. S. Flexor Carpi
Radialis.

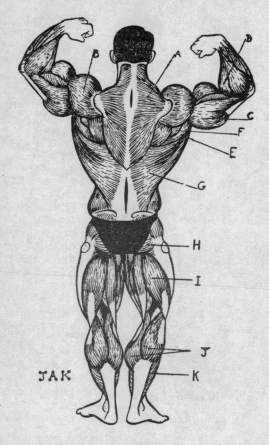

Fig. 2. Muscles of the body (rear view).
A. Trapezius. B. Deltoid. C. Triceps. D. Extensor Carpi Radialis
Longus. E. Teres Major. F. Teres Minor. G. Latissimus Dorsi.
H. Gluteus Maximus. I. Biceps Femoris. J. Gastrocnemius. K.
Soleus.

more repetitions. Rest again, and then perform ten more
repetitions of the same exercise.

When you have rested again, start with the second
exercise, which is the Deep Knee Bend. This should be
performed with a heavy object on the shoulders, if possible,
and twenty repetitions should be completed. Be sure to
breathe deeply with each repetition.

By the time you have finished this set of repetitions, you
should be breathing fairly heavily, particularly if the weight
on your shoulders is heavy, and you should follow straight
away with twenty reps of the Chest Stretch.

Rest a minute or two, and then follow on with the Deep
Knee Bend again, followed by the Chest Stretch.

The other two exercises are also done in sets of three,
completing the three sets of Chins before going on with the
three sets of Russian Knee Bend.

Follow the resistance courses in the same way. Three
sets of the full number of repetitions given in the schedule,
and always complete the three sets of the exercise before
passing on to the next exercise. The only exception is in the
barbell course, where the three sets of the Straight Arm
Pullover should be performed alternately with the three
sets of the Squats as described above in the case of the Deep
Knees Bend and the Chest Stretch.

Results are guaranteed from these bulk courses, and
training on similar lines many men have gained as much
as eight pounds in a single month, while Roger E. Eells, of
Colombus, Ohio, one of the early experimenters with this
system, training on a routine very similar to that advocated
in the barbell course, gained 25 lb. in twenty-eight days.

The main thing is to use heavy enough resistance to make
the exercises really work. Then get three square meals a day,
plenty of milk and plenty of rest and results will surely
follow.

CHAPTER VII

SCHEDULE OF WEIGHTS AND REPETITIONS

To be successful, all systems of exercise must be progressive. Day by day, week by week, month by month they must become harder to perform. Only in that way can the muscles grow and strengthen.

If exercise alone made a man big and strong, then the most muscular men in the country today would be postmen, who spend most of their working day walking the streets, or coalmen, who carry hundredweight sacks of coal often for very long distances.

But although postmen are often very fit, and coal-men are stronger than men in sedentary jobs, that is usually about as far as they go. Neither becomes as fit and big and strong as physical culturists because the amount of exercise and work remains more or less the same every day and never increases. They become strong enough to do their jobs and no more.

That is why a man who follows free exercise rarely becomes outstandingly strong and muscular, because it is so difficult to make free exercise progressive. Up to a point you can increase the difficulty of the exercises, and after that you must rely for progressing on adding more repetitions.

Indian wrestlers are said to practise nothing but free exercises in their training, and they certainly achieve some remarkable results, becoming very large, though they are not noted for outstanding muscularity, and they spend a great deal of time in training.

One of the greatest Indian wrestlers to come to this country, for instance, was Gama, who made his appearance here just before the First World War. Gama was 5 ft. 9 in. in height, with a 48-in. chest, $17\frac{1}{2}$-in. biceps, 19-in. neck and 29-in. thighs. I have no record of his waist measurement, but it is probably quite large.

A man of similar build in modern-day wrestling is Bert Assirati, and both use the Deep Knees Bend in training as a key exercise, but while Assirati will perform only ten repetitions with a 500-lb. barbell across his shoulders, Gama, in his heyday, would do from 1,500 to 2,000 repetitions without resistance.

Gama's normal day's training would find him rising at four or five in the morning, and bathing and praying. Then he would rub his body with mustard oil to assist perspiration and go through his deep-knee-bend routine, interspersed with a few hundred press-ups. He would perform these exercises, known as *Baithaks* and *Dunda* respectively, in groups of fifty to a hundred at a time.

Breakfast of almonds with milk and sugar was followed by massage for three-quarters of an hour. Wrestling practice commenced at nine against specially selected opponents for a couple of hours, followed by a rest and the main meal of the day at twelve.

Half past two would find him doing more press-ups and deep knee bends, followed by heavy manual work of some nature. A two- or three-mile run would finish the training of the day.

Later he would consume a tremendous meal consisting of cooked lentils, unleavened bread and milk. Indian wrestlers are reputed to drink from three to six quarts of milk during a day's training, which no doubt accounts in part for their heavy stature.

It can be seen, therefore, that free exercise can have as much effect as weight or cable training, but only if you are prepared to give up the whole day to it. For those people who have a job to follow and must regard physical training as a spare-time occupation, undoubtedly training with apparatus is the only answer. And why not, in view of the fact that the results that follow are quicker, easier, and better than the results of free exercise?

This book is written for beginners, and throughout it is assumed that you have never touched a barbell before, that you have exercised rarely, if ever. For that reason, the first course given is a free one, without apparatus. If followed exactly as laid down it will tone up the muscles, bring new fitness and health and improve the appearance. But it will not, by itself, bring great muscularity.

For the best results, if you are a complete novice, you should follow the free exercise course for a month before taking up any of the other three courses. If you are already in good athletic trim from some other sport or exercise, you can start straight away on one of the resistance courses.

The following schedules of repetitions and suggested poundages will show you how to work out. The free exercise course should be followed daily. The weight and cable courses every other day, or seven times a fortnight. Thus you will work out Monday, Wednesday and Friday, the first week; Sunday, Tuesday, Thursday and Saturday, the second.

Increases should be made every second exercise period. For instance, in some exercises you are told to perform six repetitions, working up to twelve. In that case, do six repetitions on Monday, six on Wednesday. Then seven on Friday, seven on Sunday. Eight on Tuesday, eight on Thursday and so on. Continue until you are performing twelve repetitions, then add five or ten pounds as indicated, to the bar, or another cable to the expander and start back at six repetitions again.

Obviously the weights you will need to commence with will depend on your strength, and it is impossible to lay down any hard and fast rules. Where six repetitions are called for, you should select a weight that will just allow you to complete six repetitions in good style, and for the average beginner the weights shown will be a good guide.

After three months of resistance training, you may care to proceed to one of the specialized courses of weight reduction or weight increase, or you may continue with the routine you are following. That is entirely up to you. The specialized courses should not be followed, however, until the three months' general training has first been completed.

Each course is designed to last four weeks before the increases in poundage are made. With the cable and weight courses, there are fourteen exercise periods in four weeks, which means the weights should be increased and the number of repetitions set back on the first work-out of the fifth week.

The free exercise course should be followed every day, but one day a week should be observed as a rest day on which no exercise is done. Normally the resistance exercise courses will follow after one month, but if for any reason you decide to carry on with non-apparatus exercises only, they should be made progressive by holding heavy objects in the hands as indicated in the schedule.

After one month of free exercise and three months of general resistance exercise, you are ready to go on with the specialized courses of weight reduction or weight increase if these are necessary.

FREE EXERCISE COURSE.   *Work out every day.*

Ex.	Reps	Increase	After one month add	Weight gain	Weight reduction
1	10	1 every 2 days	—	—	10 reps
2	10	1 every 2 days	—	10 (3 sets)	25 reps
3	15	1 every 2 days	book in hand	—	50 reps
4	15	1 every 2 days	books in hands	—	50 reps
5	20	1 every day	heavy object on shoulders	20 (3 sets)	—
6	10	1 every 2 days	—	20 (3 sets)	—
7	6	1 every 4 days	chair between legs	10 (3 sets)	15 reps
8	15	1 every 2 days	books tied to feet	—	50 reps
9	15	1 every 2 days	books in hands	—	50 reps
10	25 e.p.	1 every day	partner on back	—	25 e.p.
11	6	1 every 4 days	heavy object on chest	—	20 reps
12	10	1 every 2 days	heavy object in free hand	10 (3 sets)	—

CABLE COURSE.   *Work out every other day.*

Ex.	Start with	Reps	Increase	After one month add	Weight gain	Weight reduction
1	15 lb.	10	None	5 lb.	—	10 reps
2	20 lb.	6 e.h.	1 every 2 work-outs	5 lb.	8 (3 sets)	25 reps
3	20 lb.	6	1 every 2 work-outs	5 lb.	—	25 reps
4	40 lb.	6	1 every 2 work-outs	5 lb.	8 (3 sets)	25 reps
5	60 lb.	10 e.p.	1 every 2 work-outs	10 lb.	—	20 e.p.
6	10 lb.	10	1 every work-out	5 lb.	—	50 reps
7	10 lb.	10	1 every work-out	5 lb.	—	50 reps
8	15 lb.	6	1 every 2 work-outs	5 lb.	—	25 reps
9	30 lb.	10	1 every 2 work-outs	10 lb.	8 (3 sets)	25 reps
10	30 lb.	10 e.w.	1 every work-out	5 lb.	—	50 reps
11	20 lb.	10 e.w.	1 every work-out	5 lb.	—	50 reps
12	25 lb.	6	1 every 2 work-outs	5 lb.	8 (3 sets)	20 reps
13	15 lb.	6	1 every 2 work-outs	5 lb.	8 (3 sets)	20 reps
14	15 lb.	6	1 every 2 work-outs	5 lb.	—	20 reps
15	10 lb.	10 e.l.	1 every work-out	5 lb.	—	25 reps

BARBELL COURSE.   *Work out every other day.*

Ex.	Start with	Reps	Increase	After one month add	Weight gain	Weight reduction
1	35 lb.	10	None	5 lb.	—	10 reps
2	35 lb.	6	1 every 2 work-outs	5 lb.	8 (3 sets)	25 reps
3	45 lb.	6	1 every 2 work-outs	10 lb.	—	20 reps
4	45 lb.	10	1 every work-out	10 lb.	—	25 reps
5	15 lb.	10	1 every work-out	2½ lb.	8 (3 sets)	25 reps
6	35 lb.	10	1 every work-out	5 lb.	—	25 reps
7	35 lb.	6	1 every 2 work-outs	5 lb.	10 (3 sets)	20 reps
8	25 lb.	10	1 every work-out	5 lb.	—	50 reps
9	25 lb.	10	1 every work-out	5 lb.	—	50 reps
10	50 lb.	10	1 every work-out	10 lb.	8 (3 sets)	25 reps
11	60 lb.	10 e.p.	1 e.p. every 2 work-outs	10 lb.	—	25 e.p.
12	50 lb.	6	1 every 2 work-outs	10 lb.	10 (3 sets)	20 reps
13	None	10	1 every work-out	5 lb.	—	50 reps
14	15 lb.	10	1 every work-out	5 lb.	—	50 reps
15	45 lb.	10	1 every work-out	10 lb.	—	20 reps

DUMB-BELL COURSE. *Work out every other day.*

Ex.	Start with	Reps	Increase	After one month add	Weight gain	Weight reduction
1	5 lb. each	10	1 every work-out	5 lb. each	—	10 reps
2	30 lb.	6	1 every 2 work-outs	5 lb.	8 (3 sets)	25 reps
3	20 lb. each	6	1 every 2 work-outs	5 lb. each	10 (3 sets)	20 reps
4	5 lb. each	6	1 every 2 work-outs	2½ lb. each	—	20 reps
5	15 lb. each	10	1 every work-out	5 lb. each	—	25 reps
6	20 lb. each	10 e.p.	1 every work-out	5 lb. each	—	25 reps
7	20 lb. each	6	1 every 2 work-outs	5 lb. each	10 (3 sets)	20 reps
8	30 lb.	10	1 every work-out	5 lb.	—	25 reps
9	5 lb. each	10	1 every work-out	2½ lb.	—	50 reps
10	25 lb.	6	1 every 2 work-outs	5 lb.	—	20 reps
11	None	10	1 every work-out	5 lb.	—	50 reps
12	7½ lb. each	10	1 every work-out	2½ lb. each	—	50 reps
13	25 lb.	10	1 every work-out	5 lb. each	10 (3 sets)	25 reps
14	5 lb. each	10	1 every work-out	2½ lb. each	—	25 reps
15	15 lb. each	10	1 every work-out	5 lb. each	8 (3 sets)	25 reps

CHAPTER VIII

A COMPLETE COURSE OF
FREE EXERCISE

1. BREATHING EXERCISE (Fig. 3). Stand in an erect position, with feet astride and hands loosely by sides. Breathing in deeply, slowly raise the hands forward and up to overhead position, keeping the arms straight. Feel the ribs expanding to their utmost as you s-t-r-e-t-c-h upwards with the arms. Breath should coincide with movement, so that both end at the same moment. Pause for a second, and then, at the same speed, lower hands to sides, breathing out as you do so. Make sure the body remains upright and in good posture. This is a first-class exercise for the chest and lungs, but don't overdo it if you have never exercised before, as this may cause a little dizziness.

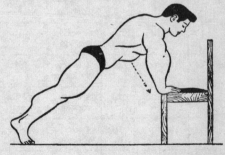

Fig. 3.   Fig. 4.

2. CHAIR DIPS (Fig. 4). Place hands on outer edges of the seat of a chair and with feet on the floor, extend the body back in a straight line. Lower face to chair seat with elbows

out at right angles to body. Walk the feet back to make sure the body is fully extended. This is the starting position. Pushing on hands, slowly raise the body to locked arms, making sure the body remains rigid, and does not bend in the middle. Then slowly lower to starting position. Start with ten reps, work up to twenty.

3.   SIDE BEND (Fig. 5). Stand erect with feet about twelve inches apart and hands by sides. Tuck right hand under right armpit and bend to the left, extending left hand down calf as far as it will go. When you have reached as far as you can, return slightly and bounce down again,

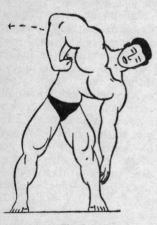

Fig. 5.

Fig. 6.

trying to go just that little further. Come to upright position, tucking left hand under left armpit and simultaneously straightening right arm. Repeat movement to the right. This is one repetition. It is important to make sure that the trunk remains in a line with the body and does not swing forward or turn towards the side to which you are bending.

Legs must remain straight and hips firm. Start with fifteen reps and work up to twenty-five.

4. TRUNK TWISTING (Fig. 6). Stand with feet astride and hands on hips. Keeping the hips firm and the legs straight, turn the body as far to the left as possible. Bounce once to complete the movement, then repeat to right. This is one repetition. Commence with fifteen reps and work up to twenty-five.

5. DEEP KNEE BEND (Fig. 7). Stand with feet together and toes pointing at an angle of ninety degrees. Place hands on hips. Rise on toes, stretching up as far as you

Fig. 7.

can, then bend knees, lowering body till you are sitting on heels. Knees should be turned well outwards and, to help preserve balance, keep eyes fixed on a spot on the wall a little higher than your head. Rise to tip-toe, straightening legs, and then lower heels to commencing position. Make sure that the movement is performed evenly, and particularly that the body is lowered into the knees bend and not dropped. Don't allow the body to tip forward, and keep the back flat throughout. Twenty reps, working up to forty.

6. CHEST STRETCH (Fig. 8). This must be carried out immediately after the Deep Knee Bend: if performed while still breathing heavily, has a most beneficial effect on the chest. Rest hands at shoulder width apart on a convenient mantelpiece, shelf or ledge which should be about shoulder high. Keep legs straight, body rigid and inclining back slightly. Breathe in deeply, expanding the chest to its limit while at the same time pressing down firmly with both hands. Relax and repeat. Ten reps, working up to twenty.

7. CHINNING THE BAR (Fig. 9). A horizontal bar at arm's length above your head is necessary for this—any horizontal bar will do. Recommended are the lintel of a strong door or the branch of a tree. Reach up and grasp the bar firmly with the palms of your hands turned towards you and your hands a little more than shoulder width apart. Pull yourself up to touch the bar with your chin, and then

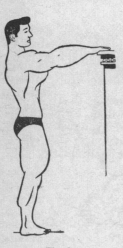

Fig. 8.

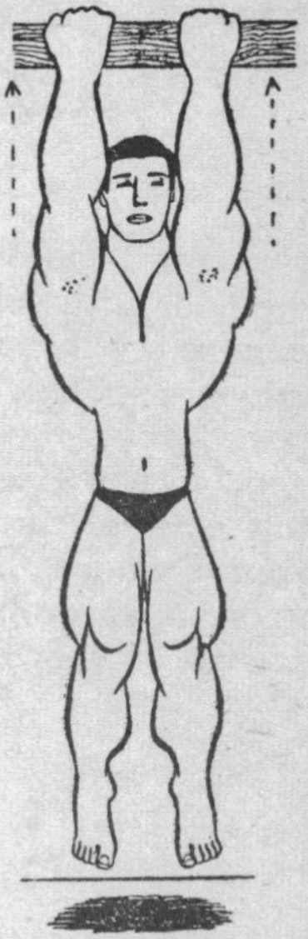

Fig. 9.

slowly lower to arm's length again. Make sure the lowering movement is slow and steady, do not drop! If you are heavily built, you will find this a tough exercise. Smaller men will find it easy. Start with six reps and work up to twelve.

8. OVERHEAD ROLL (Fig. 10). Lie flat on back with legs straight and together and arms straight at sides. Slowly

raise legs, keeping the knees stiff and toes pointed, to right angles with body, and then carry on over till your toes touch the ground behind your head. Tap the ground with them, and then slowly return to the starting position. If

Fig. 10.

you find it too difficult, assist a little by pressing down on the floor with your hands, but cut out this artificial aid as soon as possible and make it a pure abdominal movement. Fifteen reps, working up to twenty-five.

9.   SIT-UP (Fig. 11). See warning on page 18. To perform this exercise correctly, you need a willing friend to hold your feet down, but it can be managed if you tuck your toes under a wardrobe or some other heavy piece of furniture. Lie flat on your back with your feet securely anchored, and

Fig. 11.

your hands behind your head. Slowly raise the body to sitting position, keeping the legs straight and using only your abdominal muscles. Press the body forward to touch your legs with your forehead, and then lower to commencing position. Fifteen reps, working up to twenty-five.

Spencer Churchill at the peak of physical perfection

Egidio Collacico shows what a really muscular arm should look like

10. RISE ON TOES (Fig. 12). Stand with toes on a block of wood or a thick book, preferably two or three inches high, and heels on floor. Legs should be locked and straight and heels together, toes pointing out at an angle of ninety degrees. With hands on hips and legs straight, rise on toes, making sure the body is not swayed forward. Maintain balance by fixing eyes on a spot on the wall a few inches above the head. Rise slowly, taking body up to fullest extent of toes, and then lower, equally slowly. Perform twenty-five reps, then put toes together, performing another twenty-five reps with feet parallel. Then turn toes inward and heels out as far as possible, and perform another twenty-five reps. Seventy-five repetitions in all make up this exercise. Work up to fifty in each position, a total of one hundred and fifty reps. When this becomes too easy, vary the exercise by leaning forward to maintain balance and, touching the back of a chair with the finger-tips, having a heavy training partner seat himself across your hips while you perform it.

11. WRESTLER'S BRIDGE (Fig. 13). Lie flat on back with cushion or some other soft object under head. Draw feet up under thighs and get a firm position. Fold arms across chest, and roll body back until it is resting on the crown of your head and the soles of your feet. At first it may be difficult to gain this position because of lack of confidence: if so, try placing your hands on the ground beside your head to help maintain balance. As soon as possible revert to arms folded

Fig. 12.   Fig. 13.

across chest. When you have bridged successfully, lower body till it is resting on shoulders, then raise it on to crown of head again. Start with six reps, working up to twelve. When proficient, vary this exercise, by rolling the head around in a circle or supporting a light weight on your stomach in the bridge position.

12. RUSSIAN KNEE BEND (Fig. 14). Stand on the seat of a solid kitchen chair, with the left leg nearer the back.

Fig. 14.

Hold the back with the left hand for support, then slowly raise the right leg and arm and at the same time sink down on the left leg into a full deep knee bend position. The heel should not be raised from the chair, and if any difficulty is experienced in this, the heel may be supported by placing a book under it. The right leg and arm should be raised until they are parallel and horizontal, and the completion of this movement should coincide with the completion of the knee bend. Ten reps with the left leg, working up to twenty, then turn round and perform the same number of reps for the other leg.

CHAPTER IX

A COMPLETE CABLE COURSE

1. CHEST PULL (Figs. 15 and 16). Stand with the right foot about twenty-four inches in front of the left and the knees bent. Grip the handles of the expander with the palms facing outwards. Strands should be slightly below chin level and elbows straight. Pull the strands to arm's length across the chest, at the same time increasing the bend of the right knee and straightening the left leg,

meanwhile bending the body backwards. Use a light poundage and perform the movement vigorously, increasing the amount of back-bend each time. Ten reps with the right foot forward and ten with the left foot forward.

Fig. 15.

2. CURL (Fig. 17). Place right foot in one handle of the chest expander and stand erect with the feet about twelve inches apart. Grip the other handle of the expander firmly in the right hand with the palm upwards. Curl

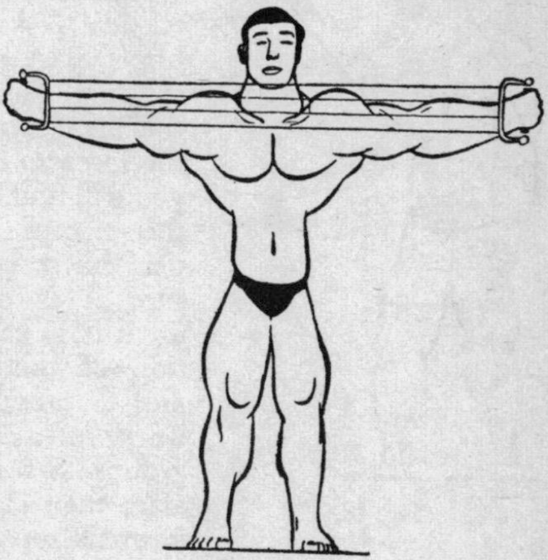

Fig. 16.

Fig. 17.

the hand to the shoulder, keeping the upper arm still and the elbow firmly in at the waist. Make sure that the forearm is the only part of the arm that moves, and that there is no back-bend or knee bending to make the pull easier. All the work must be done by the biceps, and you will find it really hard work if you perform this exercise properly.

Complete the full number of reps for the right hand, then change expander over to the left foot and hand and perform the repetitions for that hand. Start with six reps and work up to twelve. Then increase resistance.

3. TRICEPS STRETCH (Fig. 18). Stand erect with feet about twelve inches apart and hold the handle of the expander in the left hand with left arm firmly locked at

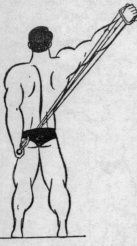

side. The right arm is bent behind head so that elbow points upwards and hand is at nape of neck, holding the second handle so that cables are approximately vertical. Without moving the upper part of the right arm or shifting the elbow, straighten the arm completely. Again it is the forearm only that moves and you will find the exercise affecting the triceps muscle strongly if performed correctly. But make sure it *is* performed correctly, for it is so easy to miss the isolation of this muscle completely and to carry a large part of the work on surrounding muscle groups. Six reps with the right arm, then change over and perform six reps with the left. Work up to twelve with each arm, then increase resistance and start back at six again.

Fig. 18.

4. THIGH STRETCH (Fig. 19). Attach one handle of the expander to a hook on the wall or alternatively slip it under the leg of some heavy piece of furniture. Place a chair at a suitable distance from the wall (experiment will show you the best position), sit on it, and tie the other handle of the expander to the right ankle with a handkerchief. Keeping the knee and thigh still, straighten the leg vigorously. The muscles at the front of the thigh must take all the work.

Repeat six times, then move handle to left ankle and perform six reps with the left leg. Work up to twelve reps and
then increase resistance.

5.   ONE-LEGGED RISE ON TOES (Fig.
20). Fasten one handle of the expander
under some heavy object on or near

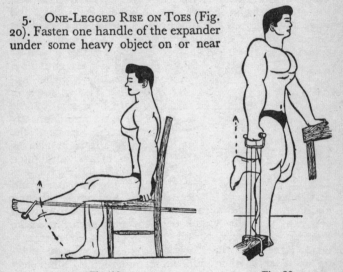

Fig. 19.   Fig. 20.

the floor. The leg of a very heavy easy chair will do. Stand
beside it, holding the other handle in the right hand. Raise
the left leg backwards and stand on the right foot only,
placing finger-tips of left hand against the back of a chair
or a wall to help support balance. Keeping the body erect
and using the expander as resistance, rise slowly on toes of
right foot, stretching up as far as possible. Lower equally
slowly. The efficiency of this exercise is greatly improved
if a block is placed under the toes as in exercise 10 of the
first course. Vary the position of the foot as in that exercise,
and perform ten reps in each position. Then change over
and work the left calf to the same number of reps. Increase
the number of reps as per the schedule of reps in Chapter
VII and then add more resistance and start at thirty with
each foot again.

6. SIT-UP (Fig. 21). See warning on page 18. Lie flat on back with one handle of expander held behind neck with both hands, and the other handle secured to your hook on the wall or under a heavy piece of furniture. Wedge the feet under a wardrobe or have somebody hold them down and then slowly rise to a sitting position (see exercise 9 of the

Fig. 21.

first course). Keep the legs straight and use only your abdominal muscles to raise the body. Go forward as far as you can, then slowly sink back to commencing position, fighting the expander all the way. Repeat ten times, working up to twenty, then add more resistance and start at ten reps again.

7. CONTINENTAL LEG RAISE (Fig. 22). With one end of the

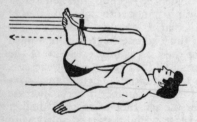

Fig. 22.

Fig. 23.

expander still fastened to the wall or heavy furniture, lie on back and fasten the other handle to both ankles with a handkerchief. The strands must go between the feet. Hands should be placed loosely at sides and not allowed to assist in the movement. Raise the legs, bending the knees and bring the thighs up to touch the chest, raising the hips off the floor. Return slowly and repeat. Start with ten reps and work up to twenty.

8. REVERSE CURL (Fig. 23). This is a humdinger for building massive forearms. Stand erect, with feet about twelve inches apart and right foot through one handle of the expander. Take the other handle in the right hand with knuckles up (i.e. the reverse of the normal curl position). Slowly curl the hand to the chest, keeping the elbow well in at the waist and the upper arm stationary. Lower just as slowly and the forearm will develop as much on the way down as it does on the way up. Six reps, working up to twelve.

9. BACK PRESS (Fig. 24). Stand erect with feet about

Fig. 24.

twelve inches apart and expander in hands across back. Elbows should rest lightly on waist, forearms be parallel to floor. Press outwards to arm's length, at the same time raising arms to shoulder level. Push forward slightly so that strands remain in contact with back and turn the hands over so that palms are facing downwards as movement is completed. Start with ten reps and work up to fifteen with usual schedule of increases.

10. SIDE BEND (Fig. 25). Place handle of expander over right foot and hold other handle in right hand with palm facing leg. Feet should be about twenty-four inches apart. Use plenty of resistance as the cables only travel a few inches! Keeping the back flat, bend over to reach as far down your left calf with your left hand as you can. Do not allow the body to lean forward or turn and make sure the hips stay firm and the legs straight. Bending the right arm will add to the difficulty of this exercise if you find it easy. Repeat ten times to the left, then change hands and bend ten times to the right. Work up to twenty reps.

Fig. 25.

11. TRUNK TWISTING (Fig. 26). Stand erect with feet about eighteen inches apart and cables held in the Back Press position. Turn the trunk to the right as far as you can, at the same time pressing the cable to arm's length as in the back press. Return to starting position and repeat to left. Make this a rhythmic, fast movement, and it will burn inches off that waistline! Repeat ten times to each side, and work up to twenty with usual schedule of increases before increasing resistance.

12. ONE ARM HIGH PULL UP (Fig 27). Place one

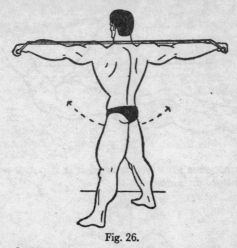

Fig. 26.

handle of the expander over your
right foot and stand erect with feet
about twelve inches apart, and cable
held in front of thigh with palm facing
in towards leg. Maintaining a strictly
erect position, raise arm, keeping
the elbow well up and out to the side.
At the conclusion of the lift, hand
should be at chin and elbow on a
level with ear. Be careful to keep
body absolutely erect when performing this movement. Six reps,
working up to twelve.

13. CHEST PULL ON BACK (Fig.
28). Lie on back with hands above
chest and arms held straight. Hold
the expander with palms turned
inwards. Keeping the arms locked,

Fig. 27.

pull the hands down and out on a level with shoulders,
breathing in as you do so. Return to commencing position,
breathing out. Six reps, working up to twelve. The efficiency

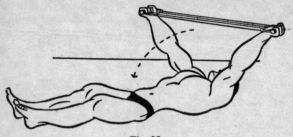

Fig. 28.

of this exercise is greatly increased if it is performed on a
low box, stool or bench.

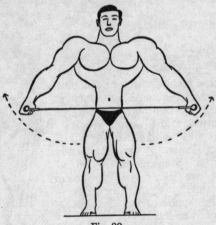

Fig. 29.

14. LATERAL RAISE (Fig. 29). Stand erect with feet
about eighteen inches apart and the expander held across
thighs on straight arms, cables passing in front of body.
Keeping the elbows locked, raise arms sideways and
upwards to shoulder level. Lower slowly, fighting the cables
all the way. Perform sometimes with the expander held
behind the body for variation. Six reps working up to twelve.

15. LEG CURL (Fig. 30). Hook expander handle to wall or under leg of heavy furniture and lie down on face with other handle tied to right ankle with handkerchief.

Fig. 30.

Raise leg from knee joint, keeping the knee and upper leg stationary. Foot should be curled over to touch thigh, and you will find the last few inches very difficult indeed. Nevertheless, fight to complete every movement, for this is a wonderful leg builder. Straighten slowly, fighting the cable all the way. Ten reps with right leg, then change over for ten with the left. Work up to twenty reps with each leg.

CHAPTER X

A COMPLETE BARBELL COURSE

1. REPETITION SNATCH (Fig. 31). Place a moderately loaded barbell on floor and stand behind it with feet about twelve inches apart. Bend the knees and crouch down firmly as if you were going to sit in a chair. Make sure the back is flat and the knees well bent. Grip the bar with hands shoulder width apart and knuckles forward. Straighten the legs vigorously as if trying to drive the feet through the floor and, using this impetus, bring the bar up high in a straight line to the overhead position, keeping it close to the body all the way. As the bar comes to arm's length above the head, turn the wrists back so that the weight is firmly supported. Don't regard this as an exercise to try

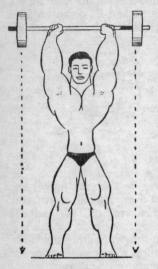

Fig. 31.

your strength: it is intended to warm you up and make you ready for the routine that is to follow. When the bar is above the head, lower it to the chest as for the commencing position of the press (Fig. 33), then let it go down gently to arm's length at the thighs. Bend the knees and crouch down until the bar almost touches the floor and then repeat the exercise. There should be ten reps in all of this movement, and it should be performed quickly and vigorously with a poundage you can handle easily.

2. TWO-HAND CURL (Fig. 32). Stand with feet astride and barbell held at thighs on straight arms with the palms of hands facing forwards. Maintaining an erect position lift the bar up till it touches the chest at shoulder level while keeping the elbows firmly tucked in at the waist. Only the forearms should move: keep the upper arms still, keep the elbows in at the waist. Resist all tendency to lean back or swing the bar up: this is a slow movement! Hold at the top, tensing the biceps, and then lower slowly to the thighs again with the same movement. Make the same amount of effort and pay equal attention to the lowering of the bar as you do to the raising of it, and your arms will develop as much from the downward movement as they do from the upward. Start with six reps, working up to twelve.

3. TWO-HAND PRESS (Fig. 33). Place a moderately loaded barbell on the floor and stand behind it as you did at commencement of first exercise. Bend the knees, keeping back flat, and grip the bar with knuckles front. Straighten

Fig. 32.   Fig. 33.

up, using the legs to take most of the work, just as in the snatch, but when the bar gets to shoulder height, pull it in to the chest, dipping the knees a little to get under the weight. At first a little difficulty may be experienced in 'turning the wrists over' to get the forearms under the weight, but a little practice with a lightly loaded bar will give you the knack. This is the clean, and is the first part of the Clean and Press.

Standing with the bell in both hands, forearms upright beneath it, and the bar resting lightly across the chest as in the illustration, you are now ready to start pressing. Feet should be about twelve inches apart, legs straight and eyes pointing straight ahead in a 'military' position. Now raise the barbell at a steady pace till it is at arm's length above the head. Pause for a second, reaching up as far as you can, then lower to chest again at same speed. Do not bend the knees, do not shift the head from the military position, and do not bend backwards at any time during this exercise.

There is no need to repeat the clean during the exercise. Press the bell six times from the chest to start with and work up to twelve reps.

4. DEEP KNEES BEND (Fig. 7). This is virtually the same exercise as number five in the first course, except that now a weight is added to give greater resistance. Carefully read the instructions given in Chapter IV before commencing. The loaded barbell should be cleaned to the chest as in the Clean and Press. Step forward about four inches with the left foot, bending the knees and straighten them vigorously, at the same time pressing the weight rapidly. As the bar passes the head, bring it back over the head to come to rest on the shoulders. When you have progressed to a high weight in this exercise, you will find you need a pair of squat racks to help you get the bar on the shoulders, as no one can jerk as much as he can squat or deep knees bend with.

When the weight is on the shoulders, it is important to round the chest, keeping the back flat and the bar well back. Keep the head up and the eyes fixed on a point on the wall above your head. Perform ten reps, working up to twenty. If you now haven't sufficient strength to jerk the bar back over your head to the clean position, squat down on flat feet and lean over sideways. Place one end of the bar on the floor and then bring your head round behind it so that you can lower the bar to the ground easily.

5. STRAIGHT ARM PULLOVER (Fig. 34). This is a good exercise for the chest and should always follow the squat or the deep knees bend, and should be performed while you are still breathing heavily. Lie on back on the floor with

Fig. 34.

lightly loaded barbell held in hands across thighs. Keeping the arms straight, raise the bar to arm's length above chest and then take it over to touch the floor behind head, breathing in deeply as you do so. Return it in same semi-circular movement to thighs, breathing out. Arms should be kept firmly locked throughout and breathing should be as deep as possible, really s-t-r-e-t-c-h-i-n-g the chest box. The efficiency of this movement is greatly increased if performed on a box, stool or bench. Ten reps, working up to twenty.

6. GOOD MORNING EXERCISE (Fig. 35). Stand erect with feet about twelve inches apart and a moderately loaded barbell across the shoulders. Keeping back flat and knees straight, bend forward at the hips and lower body until it is parallel with the floor. Without pausing, rise to upright position again, maintaining a steady, rhythmic pace. Ten reps, working up to twenty.

7. PRESS BEHIND NECK (Fig. 36). Stand erect with feet about six inches apart and a moderately loaded bar across the shoulders. Hands should be a little further apart than shoulder width, with

Fig. 35.

palms facing front. Keeping the body erect, eyes front and knees straight, steadily press bell to arm's length above head. Do not poke the head forward, hollow the back or allow the bar to wander forward over the head. Reach as high as you can, pause, then return bar to shoulders with the same unhurried speed. Six reps, working up to twelve.

8. SIDE BEND (Fig. 5). Virtually the same exercise as number 3 in the first course, except that a weight is used for greater resistance. Place a moderately loaded barbell across the shoulders and perform ten repetitions, working up to twenty.

9. TRUNK TURNING (Fig. 6). The same exercise as

number 4 in the first course, except that a moderately loaded

barbell is held across the shoulders to increase value of the exercise. Start with ten reps, working up to twenty.

10. SQUAT (Fig. 37). This is a variation of the Deep Knees Bend, but performed with a much greater weight. Feet should be flat on the floor and legs astride. Balance is easier in this version of the exercise, but nevertheless the same strict attention must be given to performance. Keep the head up and the back flat, and resist any temptation to lean forward, particularly at the lowest point of the squat, which should be when the thighs are parallel with the floor. Ten reps, working up to twenty.

Fig. 36.

11. RISE ON TOES (Fig. 12). The same exercise as

Fig. 37.

number 10 in the first course, except that a heavy barbell is held across the shoulders to increase the value of the exercise. Start with ten reps in each position working up to fifteen.

12. PRESS ON BACK (Fig. 38). Lie on back with legs straight and barbell held across chest with knuckles towards face. This is the commencing position of the exercise, but

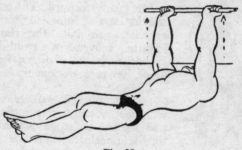

Fig. 38.

getting into it may cause a little difficulty when training alone. Personally I find the best way is to roll the barbell over the feet up to the knees while in a sitting position with the legs flat on the floor, and then to raise the barbell with the strength of hands and knees combined while at the same time rocking the body over on to the back. A gentle toss gets the bar to chest level and the legs can be straightened again afterwards. To perform the exercise, slowly press the bar to arm's length over the chest, and then lower it equally slowly to the commencing position. Start with six reps and work up to twelve. The efficiency of the exercise can be greatly increased if performed on a low bench or box.

13. LEG RAISE (Fig. 10). Similar to number 8 in the first course, but it is usually sufficient to take the legs to the vertical position when resistance in the form of barbell

plates tied firmly to the feet is added. If particularly am-
bitious, perform the overhead roll instead of the leg raise
at this point in the routine. Start with ten reps, working
up to twenty.

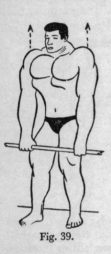

Fig. 39.

14. ABDOMINAL RAISE (Fig. 11). See warning on page
18. Similar to exercise 9 in the first
course, but performed with a light
barbell held across the chest with the
palms facing forward. The shoulders
should be well rounded during this
exercise, and both the rising and
lowering movements should be performed with the abdominal muscles
alone. Ten reps, working up to twenty.

15. SHRUG (Fig. 39). Stand erect
with feet about twelve inches apart
and barbell on straight arms across
thighs, knuckles facing forward. Keeping arms straight, raise shoulders to
highest position, squeezing them as
far as they will go. Then lower slowly,
letting them drop as far as they will
go. This is an exercise for the trapezius
and builds up those sloping shoulders
so much admired in really muscular men. Ten reps, working
up to twenty.

CHAPTER XI

A COMPLETE DUMB-BELL COURSE

1. DUMB-BELL SWING (Fig. 40). Stand with feet about
twelve inches apart and two evenly and equally loaded
dumb-bells on the floor between them. Bending the knees
and keeping the back flat, reach down and grip one in each
hand. Straightening the knees vigorously to give impetus,

swing the bells up on straight arms to over-head position.
Knees should finish straightening as bells arrive overhead.

Swing the bells down again, still keeping the arms
straight and bending knees to
allow them to travel right back
between legs to give fresh impetus to the next swing. Repeat
ten times, working up to twenty.

2.   SWINGBELL CURL (Fig. 32).
Similar to second exercise in the
barbell course, but a centrally
loaded dumb-bell is used instead
of a barbell, and the curl is performed seated to maintain strict
style. Sit on ordinary kitchen
chair with feet about twenty-four
inches apart. Hold swingbell between legs on straight arms.
Body should be inclined forward

Fig. 40.

slightly so that you can look down at the bell. Curl the weight
to the shoulders, using biceps power alone and keeping
the upper arms still. Elbows should rest on thighs and only
the forearms should move. Lower slowly, maintaining
the same strict style. Six reps, working up to twelve.

3.   DUMB-BELL PRESS (Fig. 33). Still sitting on the chair
take a bell in each hand and bring them to the shoulders
so that the palms face forward. Press slowly and steadily
to arm's length overhead as described in exercise 3 of the
barbell course. Lower and repeat. Six reps, working up
to twelve.

4.   FORWARD AND LATERAL RAISE (Figs. 41 and 29).
Standing erect with feet together and knees straight, hold
two light dumb-bells at sides with knuckles facing front.
Without bending the elbows, raise the bells forwards and
upwards to overhead position and then lower them equally
slowly. It is important not to sway the body or to swing the

bells up. The shoulder muscles must do all the work. When the bells are back at the thighs, turn the hands so that the knuckles face outwards, and raise the bells sideways to shoulder level. Stop with arms exactly on a level with shoulders, turn them over so that the palms face upwards, and then continue to raise the bells till they meet overhead. Lower to sides in the same way. Start with six reps, working up to twelve.

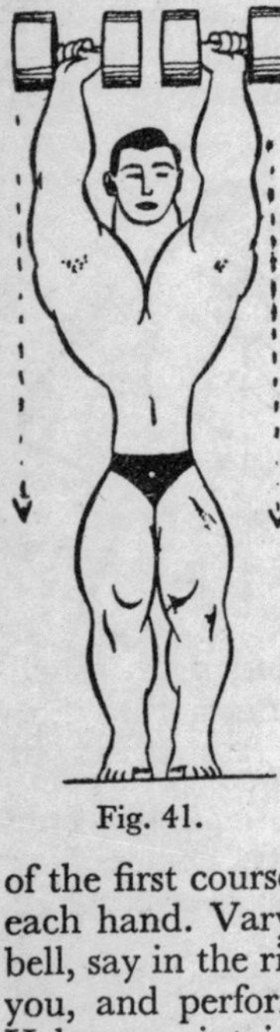

5. DEEP KNEES BEND (Fig. 7). The same exercise described in number 5 of the first course, except that a heavily loaded dumb-bell is held in each hand at the sides. As you come erect, straighten the legs forcibly so that you leap high into the air. Land on the toes and return to commencing position. Ten reps and work up to twenty.

Fig. 41.

6. RISE ON TOES (Fig. 12). The same exercise described in number 10 of the first course, except that a heavy dumb-bell is held in each hand. Vary occasionally by holding only one dumb-bell, say in the right hand, lifting left foot from floor behind you, and performing the exercise on the right foot only. Help to maintain balance by resting finger-tips of left hand on the back of a chair. Perform the number of reps for the right calf, then change the bell over to the left hand and do the same number of reps for that leg. In either case, perform thirty reps, working up to forty-five, following the instructions given in the first course as to the positioning of the feet.

7. SUPINE DUMB-BELL PRESS (Fig. 42). Performed with two heavy dumb-bells instead of a barbell, this exercise is the same as number 12 of the barbell course. Bells should be held at chest while lying on back, with knuckles out.

Press bells steadily above chest and lower slowly. Six reps to start with, working up to twelve.

8. SIDE BEND (Fig. 5). This is the same as exercise 3 of the first course, except that a heavy dumb-bell is held in the hand. First hold the bell in the right hand and perform

Fig. 42.

the stated number of bends to the left and right. Then change the bell to the left hand and perform the same number of bends each way. Start with ten reps (twenty in all) and work up to twenty reps (forty in all).

9. TRUNK TWISTING (Fig. 6). The same exercise as 4 of the first course, except that a pair of light dumb-bells is held in the hands, with the arms out-stretched to the sides at shoulder level. It is important to keep the arms level and straight and not to allow them to sink or move backwards and forwards across the body. Ten reps, working up to twenty.

10. ONE-ARM PRESS (Fig. 43). A good exercise for the arms and shoulders, this also has a powerful effect on the side muscles. With feet about twelve inches apart, take a heavy bell to the right shoulder, using both hands if necessary, and hold it there in the right hand with the palm facing forward. Get elbow well back on the hip muscles, with the forearm perpendicular. Lean over to the left and press up with the right hand at the same time. When the

bell is at arm's length, come to erect position and lower to shoulder again. Always keep your forearm perpendicular. Repeat six times with each hand, working up to twelve reps with each hand.

Fig. 43.

11. LEG RAISE (Fig. 10). Perform exactly as exercise 13 of the barbell course. Ten reps, working up to twenty.

12. ABDOMINAL RAISE (Fig. 11). Perform exactly as exercise 14 of the barbell course, except that light dumb-bells are held in the hands instead of a barbell. See warning on page 18.

13. STIFF-LEGGED DEAD LIFT (Fig. 44). Take a moderately loaded dumb-bell in each hand and hold it at the thighs with the knuckles pointing forward. Place feet together and bend forward at the hips. keeping the knees locked. Lower the bells till they almost touch the floor, then straighten up again. If performed properly, this exercise will affect the small of the back very powerfully. Repeat ten times, working up to twenty.

14. LATERAL RAISE LYING (Fig. 45). Lie on back with legs straight and arms stretched out at sides at shoulder level, a light dumb-bell in each hand and palms facing upwards. Raise the bells slowly and evenly to position over chest, keeping the elbows firmly locked. Breathe out as the bells go down, expanding chest. Breathe in as they come up again. Start with ten repetitions, working up to twenty. This exercise is improved if performed on a low stool, box or bench.

15. SQUAT (Fig. 37). The same as exercise number 5 of this course, except that dumb-bells are held in the hands at shoulders and squat is made on flat feet. Put blocks under heels if any difficulty is encountered. As you go down, press bells overhead. Knuckles should point outwards and thumbs over shoulders. Lower the bells as you rise. Ten reps, working up to twenty.

Fig. 44.

Fig. 45.

Part II

by

JIM SAUNDERS
Mr. Universe, Class II

CHAPTER I

INTRODUCTION

PART I of this book, 'Bodybuilding for Beginners' has dealt so thoroughly with the reasons *why* you should train and the results you may expect to achieve, that any attempt to enlarge further on 'general principles' would be merely repetitive.

Having read this far, the reader will now have decided which form of bodybuilding training appeals to him most, Free Exercise, Cable Exercise, or Weight Training. Your own choice will no doubt have been influenced by personal circumstances, chiefly, the time you have available for training and, perhaps more important, what you hope to achieve through your efforts.

Free Exercise schedules are excellent for maintaining a fairly high standard of suppleness, joint mobility and physical fitness but are limited insofar as muscle development is concerned.

Cable training provides plenty of resistance for the muscles and has the advantage of being very convenient for home use. The ordinary Chest Expander may be used in the bedroom, in a fairly confined space, without noise or fuss and results are fairly rapidly forthcoming.

By far the most popular form of bodybuilding work, however, is weight training, for several good reasons. First, it produces quick gains in muscular development, with strength in proportion. Second, the poundages can be adjusted to suit the very weakest *or* the very strongest men, and, thirdly, lifting weights is a *manly* pursuit, one that has been practised through the ages. Getting to grips with the weights gives an immense feeling of satisfaction—in fact, every training session will prove to be a tonic!

One further important aspect of weight training, that I almost overlooked, is that it enables one accurately to measure progress, not only in physical dimensions, but also in strength or lifting ability. With regular training you should show some improvement in strength with almost every week that passes.

If you adopt weight training simply to keep yourself in tip-top physical condition, via the employment of light to medium poundages, you will soon notice a vast improvement in your general appearance. People will begin to say how well you look and you really will be in fine fettle.

Those who take up weight training very seriously, can go on to build a prize-winning physique, with muscles to make the ordinary man's eyes pop out of his head! All you require is *perseverance*. Plan your training schedule, add weight to your barbell and dumbells as often as strength will permit, train three times a week, *regularly*, and you just cannot fail to build a magnificent body.

The chapters that follow deal exclusively with specialised weight training and the schedules recommended are guaranteed to produce the quickest possible gains in development and strength.

A full chapter is devoted to exercises for each of the main muscle groups, and you are shown how to formulate complete training programmes for all-round improvement. The rest is up to you!

CHAPTER II

HOW TO CHECK YOUR MEASUREMENTS

KEEPING a record of your bodily measurements will enable you to check your progress and avoid over-development in any particular part. Measurements are not *all-*important, of course, and your general appearance is the thing that really counts, but knowing just what your chest, biceps and other vital statistics are will help you to compare your standard of physique with that of other body-builders.

Here is the correct way to take your measurements, the

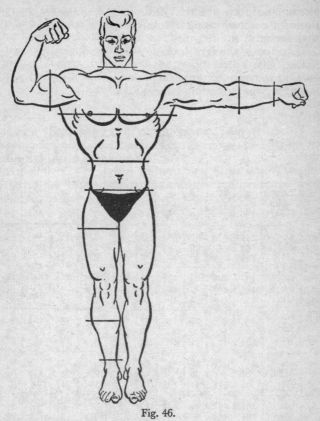

Fig. 46.

standard method used by bodybuilding champions everywhere:

Height: Barefoot, in feet and inches. *Weight:* Stripped
(If in everyday clothes, deduct 10 lbs.). *Neck:* Thinnest part,
muscles relaxed. *Chest* (expanded): Across the nipples, arms
at sides, with the tape measure level all the way round.
Fully inflate chest, tense chest and back muscles. *Waist:*
Thinnest part, body relaxed. *Hips:* Widest part, at the level

of the buttocks. *Biceps:* Bend the arm, tensing biceps strongly. See that tape measure is level all round. *Forearm:* Arm straight, fist clenched; measure round thickest part. *Thigh:* Top of the leg, thickest part, tape measure level all round. *Calf:* Thickest part, muscles tensed. *Ankle:* Thinnest part, just above the projecting bone. *Wrist:* Smallest part, just above the projecting bone. (See Fig. 46).

'IDEAL PROPORTIONS' CHART

Ht. in.	Build	Neck in.	Chest Ex. in.	Waist in.	Biceps in.	Fore-arm in.	Wrist in.	Hips in.	Thigh in.	Calf in.	Ankle in.
66	Lt.	14	40	28	13	11¼	6¼	35	20	13½	8¾
	Mdm.	15	43	29	14	11¾	6¾	36	22	14	9
	Hvy.	16	46	30	15½	12¼	7¼	36½	23	15½	9½
67	Lt.	14½	41	28	13½	11½	6¼	35½	21	14	8¾
	Mdm.	15½	44	29	14¼	11¾	6¾	36	22	14¾	9
	Hvy.	16½	46	30	16	12½	7½	37	23½	16	9½
68	Lt.	15	42	28	13¾	11½	6½	36	21½	14¼	8¾
	Mdm.	15½	44½	29	14½	11¾	6¾	36½	22½	15	9¼
	Hvy.	17	46½	30	16¼	12¾	7½	37	24	16	9¾
69	Lt.	15	42½	28	14	11¾	6½	36½	22	14½	9
	Mdm.	16	45	30	15	12	7	37	23	15¼	9¼
	Hvy.	17¼	47	31	16½	13	7½	37½	24	16¼	9¾
70	Lt.	15	42½	28	14	11¾	6¾	36½	22¼	14½	9
	Mdm.	16¼	45	30	15¼	12¼	7	37	23¼	15½	9¼
	Hvy.	17¼	47½	31	16¾	13½	7¾	38	24½	16½	10
71	Lt.	15¼	43	29	14¼	11¾	7	37	22½	14¾	9¼
	Mdm.	16½	45	30	15¼	12¼	7¼	37½	23½	15¾	9½
	Hvy.	17½	48	32	17	13¾	8	38½	24¾	17	10
72	Lt.	15¼	43	29	14½	12	6¾	37	22½	14¾	9
	Mdm.	16½	45½	31	15½	12¾	7¼	38	23½	15¾	9¾
	Hvy.	17½	49	32	17½	14	8¼	39	25	17½	10¼

Joe Abbenda of New York City, during the combined amateur and professional "Mr. Universe" contest in London, September 1963.

Joe Abbenda (left) and Tom Sansone after winning the professional and amateur divisions, respectively, of the "Mr. Universe"
contest, held in London in 1963.

CHAPTER III

MUSCULAR ARMS

I AM dealing with the arms first in these chapters on specialisation training because I believe that most body-builders prize big arms above all else. Frankly, I do not consider arms to be the most important part of the body—that distinction belongs to the abdominals, for reasons which will be explained later—but I must admit that bulging biceps and huge forearms do create an immediate impression of manly strength.

My own observations, over a period of many years, have revealed that the majority of would-be physique champions devote as much time to arm training as they spend on all other parts of the body put together! Unfortunately, results are not always proportionate to the amount of time and energy expended, usually through lack of knowledge. Arm training is quite a specialised business requiring considerable attention to detail, plus plenty of the right kind of exercise.

The idea that one good exercise for the biceps and one good movement for the triceps will ultimately produce the desired results is *out*! One reason why the quest for bulky arms so often ends in failure is that too few exercise variations are employed. There are dozens of really fine movements to choose from and, although basically they may all appear to be very much alike, as in the case of the curling movement, you can take it from me that a change now and then will help to speed the arm-moulding process. Variety is essential.

Another necessary arm-enlarging ingredient is work, *hard* work, with no letting up for aches and pains. John Grimek, who is regarded by experts as being one of the finest physical specimens the world has ever seen, was once asked how he achieved his 19½ inch biceps. 'I didn't just achieve them' said John, 'I worked for them, *slaved* in fact.' So

there's your answer: hard work, on a variety of good specialised exercises.

Let's dwell first on the Curls, which are used principally
for building the biceps. Curling is a 'must' for building
bulky biceps, but it is by no means necessary to stick to the
standard Slow Curl with barbell. In fact I recommend plenty
of dumbell movements which work the arm flexors far more
thoroughly and lend scope for variety.

Fig. 47.

Exercise 1. SEATED SINGLE ARM CURL (Fig. 47). Sit on
the edge of a bench, then, grasping a dumbell in the right
hand, allow the arm to hang straight down between the
knees, knuckles facing *forwards*. The body should be
inclined forwards and the non-lifting hand placed on the
corresponding thigh. Keeping the body motionless, raise
the dumbell up to the right shoulder by fully bending the
arm. As the bell is raised, the hand should be turned
inwards. It will make the biceps ache and produce that high
peak which looks so impressive. Return the dumbell to the
commencing position—twisting the hand outwards as you
do so.

Repetitions: 3 sets of 8—each arm.

Exercise 2. CURL ACROSS CHEST (Fig. 48). This is a very similar exercise to the foregoing movement but it gets at the biceps from a slightly different angle, thus adding to fullness of development. Standing, lean forwards from the waist and place the free hand on a bench—in the other hand you hold a dumbell, arm hanging straight down. Keeping the upper arm steady, bend the elbow and raise the dumbell

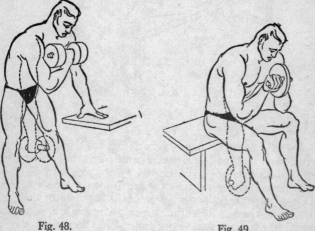

Fig. 48.   Fig. 49.

across the chest, up to the opposite shoulder. Pause very briefly, then lower the weight to the starting position. The action should be confined to the arm, so you must resist the temptation to sway the body in an effort to get the weight moving.

Repetitions: 3 sets of 8—each arm.

Exercise 3. REVERSE SWINGBELL CURL (Fig. 49). Here is an exercise that not only helps to build the biceps, but quickly adds to the bulk of the forearms. Commence by sitting on the edge of a bench, swingbell gripped with the knuckles facing forwards, arms hanging straight down, elbows resting on the inner part of the thighs. Now bend the arms, 'curling' the swingbell up to the chest. Do not allow the wrists to bend over.

Repetitions: 3 sets of 10.

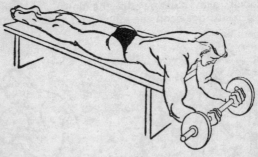

Fig. 50.

Exercise 4. PRONE BENCH CURL (Fig. 50). Here you really get down to it! Lie face down on a bench with the shoulders and arms projecting over the end. Grasp your barbell, then fully bend the arms, raising the barbell up to the shoulders. This is pure biceps leverage action and is one of the best movements known for adding quickly to upper arm measurement. Keep the weight under control and do not allow it to touch the floor as the arms are returned to the commencing position.

Repetitions: 3 sets of 10.

So much for the biceps, but we mustn't ignore the muscle that forms the back of the upper arm—the Triceps. This three-headed muscle constitutes about two thirds of the bulk of the upper arm and is strongly activated in all overhead lifting.

Exercise 5. TRICEPS STRETCH. (Fig. 51). First press a dumbell overhead with one hand and stand comfortably erect. The free hand should be folded across the chest as illustrated. Keeping the upper arm close to the head and perfectly rigid, bend the elbow and lower the dumbell down to a position behind the head. Keep the elbow pointing straight up. Now straighten the arm, making sure that the upper arm remains steady and close to the head. It requires a lot of concentration to perform this important exercise correctly, but it is vitally important that you confine the movement to the forearm only. If you lower the elbow much of the triceps building value will be lost.

Repetitions: 3 sets of 8—each arm.

Fig. 51.

Exercise 6. TRICEPS LEVER (Fig. 52). This double-handed version with dumbell loaded in the manner shown will permit quite a substantial poundage to be used. Slip the fingers under the single disc and press the weight to full arms length overhead. Lower the dumbell well down behind the head by fully bending the elbows. As with the Triceps Stretch, the upper arm must remain still with the elbows pointing well up. Steadily straighten the arms, making a point of forcibly locking the elbows to secure maximum contraction of the triceps. Incidentally, you should always check the collars before performing this exercise making sure they are really secure.

Repetitions: 3 sets of 10.

Arm training is interesting because you can really get to grips with the weights. If you use as much weight as you can correctly handle for the given number of repetitions, you will soon see a difference in the shape and size of your upper arms. It is grand to feel your biceps bulging tight inside your shirt sleeves.

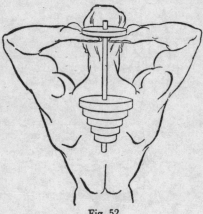

Fig. 52.

CHAPTER IV

MIGHTY CHEST

CLOTHES cannot hide the bulky contours of the deep, wide, fully-developed chest The owner looks, and has every right to be called, a 'husky'. There is no excuse whatever for the weight trainer with a poorly developed chest, or at least there won't be after reading this chapter. It is a part of the body that will readily respond to exercise, provided one is prepared to sweat a little.

As in all bodybuilding, training for chest development
must be progressive in its severity, and be applied regularly.
That is plain common sense. But the chest requires something
more. It requires variety, so a good selection of movements
should be used.

There are heaps of variations and modifications of the
standard chest-building exercises and they should all find
their place in the schedule at some time or other.

The aims of the budding 50in. chest man should be
twofold:

(1) To mobilise the thorax or rib cage, thus giving greater
expansion and increased lung power, and

(2) To develop fully the muscles covering the chest wall
—in particular the pectorals. (Note: The *latissimus dorsi*
muscles contribute a good deal to the measurement of the
chest, but they are muscles of the *back*, and will be dealt with
under 'back development' in a later chapter).

Exercise 1. BREATHING SQUAT (Fig. 53). First we will deal
with that old favourite, the Squat, in this case the Breathing
Squat. It is an exercise that should figure in all chest-
building programmes.

Fig. 53.

With a heavy barbell supported on the back of the shoulders, feet about 12 inches apart, take three full, complete breaths. Hold the last inhaled breath, bend the knees and sink down to the squat position, then return immediately upright—exhaling on the way up. Repeat with three more breaths—and so on. The heels may be raised about 3 inches on a plank or discs for a comfortable descent, but the back *must* be kept straight throughout the movement.

Repetitions: 3 or 4 sets of 12 or 15—Yes, it's meant to make you puff!

Exercise 2. PULLOVER ON BENCH (Fig. 54). Squats should always be followed by chest-mobilising exercises and there are many to choose from. A tried and tested favourite is the Pullover on Bench with Dumbells. Dumbells are more difficult to control than a barbell and for this reason are more searching in their intensity. They really stretch and mobilise the thorax (rib cage) and pectoral muscles and do much to produce that high arch to the chest. Commence by holding the dumbells on straight arms over the chest—knuckles to

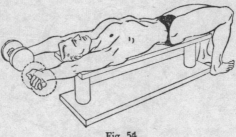

Fig. 54.

the rear. Steadily lower the arms backwards to a position behind the head—down as far as they will go, simultaneously inhaling deeply. Exhale as the arms are returned to the commencing position over the chest.

Repetitions: 3 or 4 sets of 10.

Few bodybuilders possess the amazing muscle mass and definition of Art Harris, America's "Most Muscular Man."

Caruso of Montreal

Young, handsome Dave Draper weighs an incredible 235 pounds, is capable of amazing feats of strength.

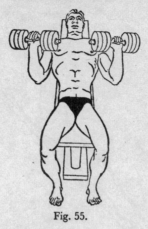

Fig. 55.

Exercise 3 (Fig. 55). This is both a mobiliser and developer. It is a 'flying' variation and scores over the straight arm lateral raise in that it permits bigger poundages to be used. The pectorals really do come under pressure in this one.

With the bells held on the straight arms over the chest, palms facing, bend the arms and lower to the position illustrated, at the same time inhaling fully. (Note the bells are held on vertical forearms, away from the body, and that the hands are turned outwards as the bells are lowered). Press back strongly to the starting position over the chest.

Repetitions: 3 sets of 12.

Exercise 4. THE DUMBELLS PRESS ON INCLINED BENCH (Fig. 56). This is another wonderful 'pec pumper'. It is especially good for the top sections of the muscle up near the collar bones. Deltoids will benefit, too.

The movement is similar in execution to exercise 3, but on an inclined bench (45 degrees), and this time the dumbells are lowered to the shoulders and not away from the body as in 'flying'. Use all the weight you can handle for 3 sets of 10.

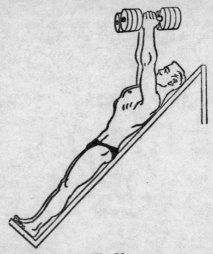

Fig. 56.

Exercise 5. THE BENCH PRESS WITH BARBELL (Fig. 57).
From the straight arm position, lower the weight fairly quickly
to touch the chest, then, taking advantage of the rebound,
press immediately to straighten the arms. Tense all the
muscles of the body and the bar will go up all the easier.

Fig. 57.

There are some good variations to the lift which may be used from time to time. These include lowering the bar to the neck, to the upper chest, to the middle of the chest, or to the lower chest. Experiment also with very wide, wide, medium and narrow grips. This last one is a killer! 3 or 4 sets of 12 or 15, with real poundages, please.

CHAPTER V

MONSTER SHOULDERS

BROAD shoulders are the hallmark of manliness and every self-respecting bodybuilder wants them—not the padded, tailor-made type, but real live shoulders, spherical bunches of muscle that appear as if they were stuck on the body as an afterthought (at least, that's the impression that well developed shoulders give to me).

You can have those broad, powerful shoulders, if you work hard. There's no secret formula that will produce herculean deltoids overnight, but a few weeks training on the exercises outlined in this chapter will thicken and enlarge your shoulders to an amazing degree. A year's specialisation can give you shoulders of championship calibre!

Knowing something about the *function* of the muscles being exercised is half the battle in modern bodybuilding, for it helps towards a better understanding of the movements involved and why it is so important to adhere to correct lifting technique.

Briefly, *very* briefly, for I do not intend to dwell overlong on technicalities, the deltoid is the muscle that covers, or 'caps' the shoulder joint. It is split into three sections, *anterior* (front), *lateral* (side) and *posterior* (rear), all sets of fibres. The chief action of the deltoid is to abduct or raise the arm sideways to a little above shoulder level—the lateral fibres being the prime movers. The anterior fibres assist in raising the arm forwards and upwards and the posterior section, as you may have guessed, draws the arm backwards. No set of fibres acts *entirely* independent of the others.

Complete development of the deltoids calls for 'satura-
tion' tactics, with specialised exercise for all three sets of
fibres. One important fact to remember is that *any* overhead
lifting movement *must* have a beneficial effect. But there
are ways and means of lifting weights aloft to isolate the
muscle activity almost exclusively to the deltoids and these
are the exercises that I am going to explain in detail.

Before proceeding further, however, take a look at some
of the kings of shoulder development, and the methods
they used to produce maximum muscle bulk. The late
Ronald Walker, who represented Britain and took second
place at weightlifting in the 1936 Olympic Games in
Berlin, possessed really enormous deltoids—huge masses of
muscle that rippled with every movement he made.
Strangely enough, Ron was relatively poor on the Two
Hands Press, an Olympic lift of a pure leverage nature
that demands great shoulder power. *Because* of his weakness
in the press, he devoted many hours of his training time to
the practice of the lift, in order to gain extra strength.
Although he never succeeded in becoming a worldbeater
at pressing, this specialised treatment rewarded Ron with
a pair of shoulders that were unmatched in the world of
strength athletics and it is doubtful if we shall ever see such
shoulders again. Incidentally, Ronald Walker was not built
for strong pressing but he excelled at the faster lifts and
created a world record on the Two Hands Snatch with a
poundage of 297½. (Unofficially he succeeded with 317
lbs. and regularly snatched over 300 lbs. in training.)

Reuben Martin of Tottenham, London, is another
famous 'shoulder' man and he, too, possesses extraordinary
strength. Reuben is a champion in many spheres of strength,
weightlifting, bodybuilding, acrobatics and 'herculean'
hand-balancing. In the latter field he performs countless
repetitions of the hand-stand press-up, a truly remarkable
feat for a man weighing around 210 lbs. and this training
no doubt accounts, in part, for his magnificent shoulder
spread.

One cannot discuss the subject of shoulder development
without mentioning Britain's greatest bodybuilder, Reg
Park—twice winner of the official 'Mr. Universe' title.

Reg is a specialist in two fields, weightlifting and body-building, and his physique just has to be seen to be believed. His 54 inch chest and 19½ inch biceps are matched by the finest pair of shoulders in the world today.

Deltoids require a lot of hard exercise if they are to achieve the fullness of absolute development. All forms of pressing are recommended, particularly pressing with dumbells. For purposes of specialisation I recommend performance of all the five exercises set out in this chapter. At least two of the movements (or variations) should figure in one's general training programme.

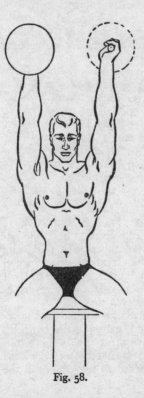

Fig. 58.

Exercise 1. SEATED DUMBELLS PRESS (Fig. 58). You will quickly discover that dumbells pack power into every deltoid fibre, and this exercise is amongst the very best. Sit comfortably upright with a couple of dumbells held at the shoulders, palms facing inwards. Take a full breath, brace the body, then press the dumbells to full arms' length overhead. Pause very briefly, and lower the bells back to the shoulders, ready for the next repetition. Do *not* lean back from the waist and be sure to press the weights well back as they travel aloft.

Repetitions: 3 sets of 8.

Fig. 59.

Exercise 2. PRESS FROM BEHIND NECK (Fig. 59). Here is a movement that adds bulk to both the lateral and posterior portions of the deltoids and is particularly recommended for speedy results. It may be performed either seated or standing, but I would suggest use of the latter style for the first month or so as it is a very severe exercise and really 'burns' the shoulders.

Commence with the barbell in the 'behind neck' position, as illustrated, gripping the bar with the hands fairly wide apart. Now press the barbell to full arms' length overhead, pushing the weight well back as it travels upwards. Be sure to lock securely the elbows in the straight position

Leroy Colbert is reputed to have the world's largest muscular arms: 20½ inches around the biceps!

Caruso of Montreal

Ray Routledge after winning the 1961 "Mr. America" contest in Santa Monica. At right, Madeline Mack, "queen" of the show.

as this last little extra push produces full muscle contraction. Return the bar to the starting position behind the head. A helpful hint in all pressing movements is to tense *all* the muscles of the body as the bar is raised overhead. A firm lifting foundation allows for a more vigorous drive with the arms and results will appear more quickly. Bear in mind also that the press is *not* a slow exercise and the bar should be elevated just as quickly as the poundage will allow.

Repetitions: 4 sets of 8.

Fig. 60.

Exercise 3. SEATED LATERAL RAISE (Fig. 60). Yes, you *may* sit down for this one, and, furthermore, you will need to lift only very light dumbells! But there is a catch in it. You will find that this is far from a restful sort of exercise.

Grasp a couple of light dumbells (try 10 pounders for a start) then sit down, allowing the arms to hang straight down at your sides. Keeping the trunk erect, steadily raise the arms sideways and upwards until they are in line with the shoulders. Pause very briefly, then reverse the action returning the arms to the sides. The lowering movement should be *controlled*, in order to maintain full contraction of the shoulder muscles. Breathe in as the weights are raised and out, through the mouth, as they are lowered.

Repetitions: 3 sets of 8.

Exercise 4. UPRIGHT ROWING (Fig. 61). Many bodybuilders regard this as an arm building exercise, which it is, but completely overlook the fact that it is also a fine shoulder-builder. It's one of the best movements known for developing the anterior (front) section of the deltoids. You will find this a most pleasurable exercise.

Fig. 61.

Grip the barbell with a 4 inch hand-spacing, arms hanging straight down in front of the body, knuckles to the front. Vigorously pull the bar up to the level of the neck, at the same time raising the elbows high. The wrists do *not* turn over. The bar should be kept in close to the body as it is raised and you must fight against the temptation to lean backwards from the waist. Lower and repeat.

Repetitions: 3 sets of 10.

Exercise 5. ALTERNATE FORWARD RAISE (Fig. 62). This is another light dumbell move; in fact, you will find it virtually impossible to handle anything *but* small poundages! Stand with your back resting against a wall, a dumbell in each hand, knuckles forward. Raise the right arm, at moderate speed, forwards and upwards to overhead. Pause briefly, then lower to the commencing position. As the right arm is lowered the *left* arm commences its upward journey. Make it a good rhythmic action —and take care not to allow the dumbells to meet at the midway position! Breathe naturally, through the mouth.

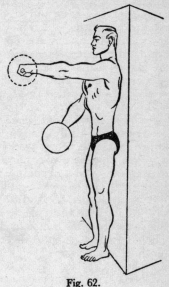

Repetitions: 3 sets of 8, each arm.

The road to successful shoulder-building is open to all, with no real secrets, except perhaps *hard work*!

Fig. 62.

CHAPTER VI

BUILDING FINE THIGHS

MOST fellows dislike specialised leg exercise in any shape or form, simply because it is tough work. It is gruelling, in fact, but like nasty medicine, it's very necessary—to make you look and feel better!

Training for increased leg development makes you feel good because it stimulates the action of the heart and lungs and therefore thoroughly conditions the body as a whole. Remember that *any* exercise that steps up the circulation and creates deep, natural respiration will do you a lot of good. For example, a few repetitions of any good weight exercise for the legs is as beneficial as road running to lick you into A.1 shape—but you have *got* to work.

Some of the largest and strongest muscles of the body are situated in the thighs and they are capable of absorbing an enormous amount of work. But they respond well to special-ised treatment and a few weeks intensified effort will pay off in the shape of heftier thighs and calves and much greater strength. Although the majority of bodybuilders prefer to slave for increased upper body musculature, some find greater satisfaction in specialising on feats that call for sheer leg strength. Some really fantastic performances have been recorded. Paul Anderson, former heavyweight weight-lifting champion of the world, made an open challenge to any man, anywhere, to duplicate his stunt on the Full Squat movement—with a handsome cash reward for anyone who succeeded. The test was as follows:

Two steel safes, with glass sides, each containing 7,500 silver dollars for all to see, were attached to each end of a thick steel bar, the whole load supported on squat stands. The lifter had to support this costly load across the back of his shoulders, perform a full knees bend (Squat) then return upright and replace the bar on the stands.

Nobody ever succeeded—except, of course, Paul himself, who demonstrated the feat every day. The weight of the safes, with dollars and steel bar, was in excess of 1,300 lbs.!

I am not suggesting for one moment that the ordinary man can rise to such heights of strength output, but I will say that you can amaze yourself with your leg-power feats, in just a few weeks, if you apply yourself diligently to the task. Even the very light men should ultimately be handling 200 lbs. or more in the Squat exercise.

In addition to developing good legs, the various forms of Squat exercise will help you to make all-round gains in muscularity. Men who are lacking in bodyweight, are recommended to include 3 or 4 sets of 15 repetitions of the Full Squat or Breathing Squat in their training schedule and results will appear very quickly.

Already it must be apparent to readers that the Squat is a very important exercise. It's the *key* exercise in leg culture, but it's not enough in itself and other specialised movements must be incorporated into the training programme if the legs are to be built to the pitch of perfection. As we have talked so much about squatting, we will start with that basic exercise first:

Fig. 63.

Exercise 1. FULL SQUAT (Fig. 63). This is probably the most popular of all weight-training exercises and it is certainly one of the most effective. Commence with the barbell supported across the back of the shoulders, feet comfortably apart, heels raised a couple of inches on a plank or barbell discs.

Keeping the back straight, bend the knees and sink down to the full squat position. Pause very briefly, then return upright. Inhale deeply before the legs are bent and exhale on the upward journey. The important thing is to keep the back flat, all the time, and this is made easier if you incline the body forwards slightly, from the waist.

Raw beginners are best advised to perform only *half* squats during the first couple of weeks of training, gradually increasing the range of the leg movement as strength and technique improve. Looking up at a point a little above eye level will also assist one in keeping the back straight.

Repetitions: 3 or 4 sets of 15.

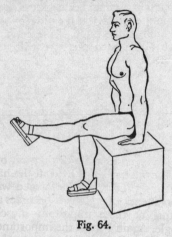

Fig. 64.

EXERCISE 2. SINGLE LEG EXTENSIONS (Fig. 64). This movement quickly sharpens the definition of the thigh muscles and also builds them to massive proportions. It is particularly effective in developing the *vastus medialis*—that bulge of muscle on the inner side of the thigh just above the knee. Iron Boots or dumbells should be strapped to the feet. Sit on a fairly high bench, lift one foot from the floor then vigorously straighten the leg, strongly tensing the muscles of the thigh as you do so. Steadily lower the foot to the commencing position, then immediately repeat the action.

Repetitions: 3 sets of 10—each leg.

EXERCISE 3. 'HACK' SQUAT (Fig. 65). This is a variation of the famous 'Hack' lift, which was invented by that great, old-time strong-man, Georges Hackenschmidt. The

Fig. 65.

Hack Squat is really nothing more than an ordinary Full Squat, except that the barbell is held in the hands, behind the body, close to the buttocks. Performed with the heels raised a couple of inches on a plank it becomes a super thigh developer, getting at these important muscles from an entirely new angle. Again I stress the importance of keeping the back straight. Use all the weight you can handle in this one.

Repetitions: 4 sets of 8.

Exercise 4. LEG CURL (Fig. 66). Squatting in its various forms will do much to develop the hamstrings which are situated on the back part of the thigh, but a specialised exercise for this part of the anatomy will make for snappier progress and a more shapely appearance. You don the iron boots again for this one. (If you don't possess this luxury piece of apparatus, remember it is an easy matter to strap a dumbell to the foot). The action is almost self-explanatory. Vigorously flex the knee, raising the foot as high as possible to the rear. Endeavour to bend the knee just a little more fully with each repetition and you won't need to be told where the biceps of the thigh are situated, you will feel them 'burn'!

Fig. 66.

If you are at all subject to cramp, it is a sound plan to massage the backs of the thighs immediately after performing this rather tough exercise. It will help to prevent soreness, but if this should occur, don't worry, as it will wear off after a few days.

Repetitions: 2 sets of 10—each leg.

Exercise 5. STRADDLE LIFT (Fig. 67). Many instructors consider this movement, quite erroneously, to be a strength builder, and nothing more. In actual fact it is a fine muscle *developer* as well, giving firm lines to the upper sections of the thighs and hips. Stand *astride* the barbell, then, gripping it 'fore and aft' as illustrated, rise to the erect position. The action thereafter consists of bending the knees and lowering the bar about 15 inches, then returning upright. Really respectable poundages can be handled in this manner, but *keep that back straight!*

Repetitions: 3 sets of 10.

Fig. 67.

CHAPTER VII

CALF CULTURE

UNLESS you are naturally endowed with big, shapely calves, sooner or later you will find it necessary to specialise on this oft-neglected part of the anatomy—that is if you wish them to remain in proportion with the rest of your physique.

Calf building is not easy, but it's not *all* that difficult, if you use the right exercises and perseverance. A fact often overlooked is that a gain of half an inch on the calves is proportionate to, say, a couple of inches or more on the chest.

The muscles that make up the calf, the main bulk arising from the *gastrocnemius*, *soleus* and *tibialis anterior*, are of the long, thin variety, built for stamina rather than size. Calves are constantly in use, in walking, standing, running, etc. and are therefore highly conditioned and quite accustomed to being vigorously exercised. It follows that really severe training measures are needed to produce worthwhile gains in development. The secret is to use plenty of resistance *plus* a high number of repetitions *and* a good assortment of exercises.

Some of the world's best built men possess wonderfully shaped calves, stretching the tape measure to 18 or 19 inches! They didn't start off with calves so big, but built them up over a period of years, using countless repetitions and untiring perseverance. The great Steve Reeves, owner of one of the finest pair of legs this world has ever seen, devoted hours on end to calf culture. At one period, just prior to winning the coveted 'Mr. Universe' title, he performed more than 1,000 repetitions of the 'heels raising' exercise a day—the free movement without weights. This was additional to the specialised weight training exercises in his regular work-out. Steve's calves measured 18¼ inches, matched with 18¼ inch biceps and a 52½ inch chest!

Basically, all the various calf building exercises look alike —rising on to tip-toe, against the resistance of a barbell. The action *is* invariably the same, but there are ways and means of bringing pressure to bear on different parts of the muscle, thus ensuring full and complete development. One very important point to remember is to work the calf muscles through their full range of action, which means rising fully on to tip-toe and thrusting the heels well down on the return journey. Massage is helpful, particularly in stubborn cases. Press the thumbs deep into the 'belly' of the calf, then work them in a circular motion to cover all parts of the muscle. A couple of minutes massage to each lower leg, after training, will loosen them up wonderfully and help to produce the gains you seek.

Exercise 1. STANDING HEELS RAISE (Fig. 68). This is the standard calf building movement—the basic exercise that should appear in all calf routines. Stand with a barbell supported across the back of the shoulders, feet about 15 inches apart. Rise fully on to tip-toe, pause very briefly, then return the heels to the floor. This should be a vigorous movement and it helps if you endeavour to rise higher on the toes with every repetition. This ensures full muscle contrac-

Muscles replaced music at Carnegie Hall in New York City, March 1951, where the "Mr. Strength and Health" contest was held. Winners, l. to r., Irvin Koszewski (2nd), Melvin Wells (1st), Al Berman (3rd).

The winner of a professional "Mr. Universe" title, Harold Poole is the most sensationally developed teenager in America.

Fig. 68.

tion. After a couple of weeks, the muscle action can be intensified by performing the same movement with the toes resting on a thick plank.

Repetitions: 4 sets of 15.

Exercise 2. SEATED CALF RAISE (Fig. 69). Yes, you may sit down for this one, but I can assure you that the muscle work is every bit as severe. Sit on a chair or bench, holding a barbell across the knees. The toes should rest on a thick plank or couple of barbell discs. Simply raise the heels as high as possible from the floor at the same time tensing the calf muscles hard. Sitting down to it isolates the muscle action exclusively to the lower legs and you will be surprised how tough a few repetitions, with a reasonable poundage, can be.

Repetitions: 3 sets of 15.

Fig. 69.

Fig. 70.

Exercise 3. CALF WALKING (Fig. 70). This sounds a peculiar sort of exercise but it involves the commonest of all movements known to man—walking—but with a difference. The difference is in the form of a heavy barbell which is held across the back of the shoulders. Walk round your training den with an exaggerated heel-and-toe action, then complete the session by walking high on tip toe for about a couple of minutes. It's tough work, mighty tough, but really terrific for moulding powerful calves. Three minutes walking in all should prove sufficient.

Fig. 71.

Exercise 4. SINGLE CALF RAISE (Fig. 71). This is the same old movement—but applied to one leg at a time. Stand with a heavy dumbell held in one hand, the opposite hand resting on a chair-back, for balance. Raise one foot clear of the floor. Now perform a single leg calf raise, getting up as high as possible on the toes. It is quite a difficult exercise but one that will pay off handsomely in the shape of better-looking calves.

Repetitions: 2 sets of 10—each leg.

CHAPTER VIII

SUPER ABDOMINALS

"WHAT a wonderful physique that fellow's got!' Over-hearing this remark made by a blonde to her friend at a swimming pool, I cast my eyes in the direction of the body responsible for the feminine heart-flutterings.

The possessor of the 'wonderful physique' had little or no claim to bulkiness, in fact, from bodybuilding standards, he would be called downright skinny—but there could be no denying his development was *attractive*. He had an *interesting* physique and I noticed that most swimmers and sunbathers present favoured him with more than a casual glance.

'Why', I asked myself, 'should this fellow create such an impression?' A closer examination revealed that he not only had good all-round muscular definition, but a *wonderful set of abdominals*, the finely chiselled sections being plainly visible even in complete relaxation. Many bulkier physiques were on view that day but not one mid-section could com-pare with that of our friend, who completely, but un-wittingly, stole the limelight.

Well-developed abdominals are a sure sign of a high stan-dard of physical fitness. Few men possess naturally well-defined abdominals and the deep corrugations of muscle can only be achieved through regular and persistent exercise routines. The principal action of the abdominals is to draw the ribs closer to the pelvis by bending the body forwards, but they also assist in exhalation (breathing out). Remember, that, when you wish to display your abdominal definition, breathe out, then forcibly tense the mid-section. If you have trained hard, the muscles will stand out clearly, hard and rocklike.

Weights are unnecessary for many of the popular abdom-inal exercises as one's own bodyweight can be made to pro-vide the necessary resistance and this is quite ample—until you reach championship standards. To assess whether or not you have done sufficient repetitions, you must consider your own physical reaction. If the last few repetitions are difficult, but still manageable, then you are on the right lines. If, however, you find that you can carry out all the given number of repetitions easily, without undue strain, then you are *not* working hard enough, and more repetitions should be used—or a different abdominal movement.

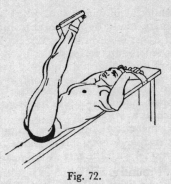

Fig. 72.

Exercise 1. OVERHEAD ROLL—ON INCLINE (Fig. 72). For this, and exercise 2, you will require an abdominal board. A plank of wood about 6 feet in length will serve the purpose. Rest one end of the plank on a suitable support to give an incline of approximately 40 degrees. Lie on the board, head at the top, and reach over and grip the top of the plank to prevent yourself from slipping down. Now, raise the legs up just as high as they will go—breathing out as you do so—pause briefly, then return to the starting position. As your abdominals grow in strength, you should also lift the hips from the plank, after the legs have been raised. This makes it a really tough abdominal improver and a great favourite with the champions.

Repetitions: 2 or 3 sets of 10.

Exercise 2. SIT-UP—ON INCLINE (Fig. 73). The movement you have just performed is particularly good for the lower

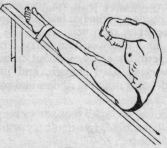

Fig. 73.

sections of the abdominal wall. Exercise 2, the Sit-up,
develops the *upper* sections but also has a good tonic effect
on the abdomen as a whole.

The action is exactly the reverse of what you have just
done. The board should remain at the same 40 degree angle
but this time you lie with the feet at the head of the board,
(secured in position with a strap). Clasp your hands behind
the head, *round the back* and rise to the sitting position,
endeavouring to touch the knees with your forehead.
Steadily unroll to the starting position. Remember to
breathe *out* as you sit up and *in* as the body is lowered.
Maybe you are wondering why you are advised to round the
back? The reason is because this isolates the muscle action
more exclusively to the abdominals. If you kept the back
straight throughout the sit-up, the thighs would be doing
most of the work.

Repetitions: 2 or 3 sets of 10.

Fig. 74.

Exercise 3. ALTERNATE KICK (Fig. 74). This is almost as much a leg as an abdominal exercise, but it helps in the general tummy toughening process and is a fine physical conditioner. Your iron boots should be donned and the commencing position is lying on the back, on the floor, with the hands clasped behind the head. Alternately draw each leg up to the abdomen, then vigorously re-straighten, lowering the foot to the floor after each repetition. When you become tough, you may manage to keep the feet clear of the floor, all the time, but don't try it during the early stages of your training.

Make it a rhythmic movement for 2 sets of 15 reps.

Fig. 75.

Exercise 4. SIDEBEND, WITH DUMBELL (Fig. 75). This is specially for the oblique abdominals—the muscles on the sides of the trunk. Grasp a 20 lb. dumbell in one hand, then stand with the body erect, feet about 15 inches apart. Bend the trunk as far down to the right as the mobility of the spine will allow, straighten up, then down to the *left* as far as possible, and so on, at moderate tempo. Be sure not to lean forwards as the trunk is bent for this would rob the obliques of much valuable exercise. Breathe naturally, through the mouth.

Repetitions: 30 with the dumbell in the right hand, 30 in the left.

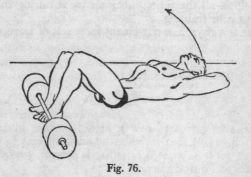

Fig. 76.

Exercise 5. SIT-UP, WITH KNEES RAISED (Fig. 76). A variation of the sit-up movement you have already performed, but this time you dispense with the inclined board, and place the feet under a barbell, with the knees raised, as shown. Clasp the hands behind the head, then sit up, not forgetting to round the back, bit by bit, as you do so. Thrust the head well forwards over the knees, then unroll to the lying position. Breathe *out* as you sit up.

Repetitions: 3 sets of 10.

Exercise 6. CONTINENTAL ROLL (Fig. 77). This is the final specialised abdominal exercise, but one of the very best. Why it should be called the 'continental' roll I do not know, as top physique men everywhere use it.

With iron boots strapped to the feet, lie on your back, hands at sides, feet drawn up close to the buttocks. Keeping

Fig. 77.

the knees fully bent, lift your feet from the floor, then the hips, and roll over to touch your shoulders with the knees. Reverse the movement, lowering the feet to the floor—still with the knees fully bent. This is another exercise that can be performed on the inclined board, but only when your abdominals are very strong.

Repetitions: 2 sets of 10.

Some bodybuilders find abdominal exercise boring, simply because it involves fairly high repetitions and the fact that results cannot be measured in inches (except in cases of weight reduction). But whether the work appeals to you or not, *it has got to be done*. Your *physique, strength, general fitness* and *health* will quickly benefit.

CHAPTER IX

BRAWNY BACK

WHEN it comes to lifting weights, a man is as strong as his back. If his back is weak, then he cannot be a strong man, for it's the back that bears the brunt of the work in any lifting.

Fortunately, almost any weight training exercise, performed standing up, will activate the back muscles to a certain degree. But, if you are to be *really* strong, then some specialised movements must be performed to pack bulk and power into the many muscles, most of which are large ones, that go to make up the hind surface of the human body.

The better to illustrate the task before us, let us take a brief look at the anatomy of the back. First there is the *trapezius* muscle. Although situated in the back, the 'traps' of the well-developed strength athlete are perhaps best viewed from the front, where they will be seen sloping from the sides of the neck down to the shoulders. They form the natural 'slope' to broad shoulders. Their chief function is to elevate, depress or brace the shoulders backwards.

The *latissimus dorsi* muscles also appear very impressive when viewed from the front. They are the large V-shaped 'under arm' muscles that give the wonderful spread to the chest—and back. *Everybody* wants, and admires big 'lats'!

Of all the major back muscles, the most important from a strength and fitness point of view are the *erector spinae*, but often they are neglected, simply because they are not built, or ideally situated, for display. They are seen as columns of muscle on either side of the spine in the lumbar (lower) region of the back.

If you desire *strength* proportionate to the *size* of the muscles you aim to achieve, the lower back must be thoroughly exercised and not left in neglect. A little Dead Lifting, standard or stiff-legged, is all that is really necessary, though other exercises may be used to provide variation.

The first couple of exercises recommended for full back development are not weight training movements at all—your own bodyweight will provide *ample* resistance—in fact, in the early stages it may prove more than enough!

EXERCISE 1. CHINNING THE BAR (Fig. 78). This is a great old favourite but few bodybuilders realise its vast potentialities as a back-broadener. Grasp a fixed overhead bar, raise the feet clear of the floor, body hanging at full stretch. The hands should be a little more than shoulder-width apart. Now pull up vigorously, to touch the bar with your chin—or as near as you can—*further* if possible. Lower to full arms stretch, without returning the feet to the floor, ready for the next repetition. Breathe *out* as you pull up and *in* as the body is lowered.

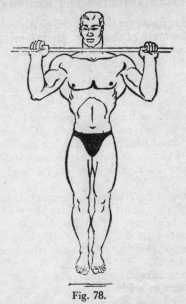

Fig. 78.

Repetitions: Perform as many as you can, for three sets, with a one-minute rest between each set.

Exercise 2. CHINNING BEHIND NECK (Fig. 79). This is another great *latissimus dorsi* builder and also has a wonderful effect on the *trapezius* muscles which lie on the back of the neck and shoulders. Commence as you did with the last exercise, hanging full stretch, arms straight. Now pull up, as before, but this time nod the head forwards and endeavour to touch the bar with the back of your neck. It's *not* an easy movement but is really great for piling on development—fast!

Repetitions: Perform as many as possible, for three sets, with a one-minute rest between each set.

Exercise 3. TWO HANDS DEAD LIFT (Fig. 80). This is the greatest power-promoting exercise ever devised. It is simply

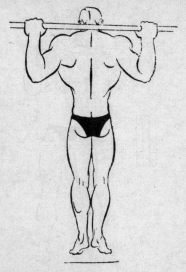

Fig. 79.

great for strength increase, has a tremendous toning effect on all the body, and can be relied upon to assist in weight gaining. A fairly good poundage should be used right from the very start and I suggest you try one-and-a-half times your own body weight—just to see how things go. Bend down and grasp the bar with the arms and back straight, knees half bent, head up, chin in. Now, simply stand up with the barbell by vigorously straightening the legs. As you come erect, brace the shoulders well back and thrust the chest forwards. Lower the weight to the floor by reversing the action.

A useful hint, and one that will enable you to raise bigger than normal poundages, is to grasp the bar with one hand facing forwards and the other hand facing the rear. In this manner the bar cannot easily release itself from your grip. Note, also, that the arms should be exactly shoulder-width apart. A wide hand spacing is uncomfortable and impracticable.

Fig. 80.

Dead lifting builds powerful back musculature and is particularly useful for developing the *erector spinae* muscles which appear as columns on either side of the spine.

Repetitions: Three sets of 10.

Fig. 81.

Exercise 4. BARBELL ROWING (Fig. 81). Rowing, in its

various forms, is wonderful for developing the *latissimus dorsi* and back muscles generally and also does much to improve arm bulk. Some bodybuilders prefer the standard barbell rowing movement while others seem to reap richer rewards from the single dumbell move. I will describe both, commencing with the barbell.

Grasp the bar with a fairly wide grip, then, with feet apart, lean forwards from the waist, allowing the arms to hang straight down. Keep the back flat. Give a big heave and pull the bar up to touch the chest then immediately lower the weight to straight arms. You may find it necessary to sway the body a little to keep the weight in motion, particularly when you are handling respectable poundages, but don't overdo the body action or you will be robbing the arms and upper back of valuable developmental work. Breathe in as the bar is raised and out as it is lowered to straight arms.

Repetitions: 3 sets of 12.

Fig. 82.

Exercise 5. SINGLE ARM ROWING (Fig. 82). A great favourite and one that gives plenty of satisfaction as you can really feel the powerful back muscles responding to 'treatment'. This exercise is rapidly gaining in popularity, as well it may, for it is a result-getter *par excellence*. Adopt the usual rowing position (back and legs straight) but this time with the head resting on the forearm on a table or chair-back (see illustration). Viciously pull the dumbell up to the shoulder, then shrug the shoulder well back to bring the smaller muscles of the shoulder girdle into play. Lower the weight to the commencing position, controlling it on the way down.

The important thing is to keep the head firmly in place across the arm, thus isolating the muscle action to the upper back and shoulder girdle. Use a heavy dumbell, one that will really make you work—and you can then look for results after a matter of days!

Repetitions: 3 sets of 12—each arm, in alternate sets.

CHAPTER X

TRAINING FOR ALL-ROUND PHYSICAL IMPROVEMENT

THE preceding chapters list quite a large number of specialised weight training exercises, showing how they should be performed—with the best number of repetitions to suit the average bodybuilder. It must be stressed, however, that these chapters do not provide complete training schedules in themselves and to use one set of exercises only, say for the arms, would result in failure.

Some fellows labour under the impression that by devoting all their training time to just one part of the body they can achieve outsize proportions, but they are wrong. It is just not possible to build, say, 18 inch biceps, leaving the rest of the body in a state of under-development, yet that is just what some beginners set out to achieve. They *slave* on arm-building movements, neglecting the rest of their body, then complain bitterly when they discover that their arm measurement will not budge above a certain figure. Here is the reason.

Muscles can be *over*-trained (from a developmental point of view) and, after a certain amount of over-specialisation, the muscle fibres will toughen up and become stringy. From then on they may increase in *strength*, but will not become *larger*. The better to illustrate this point, one has only to observe the leg muscles of the long distance runner.

With the tremendous amount of exercise they receive, one would expect them to be muscular to an extreme, yet the reverse is the case. The champion 'distance' man has comparatively slim legs, *overworked* as far as muscle *building* is concerned.

Hard work is, of course, necessary, but the body as a *whole* must be trained, with perhaps a little extra attention to the weaker parts of one's physique. Muscles will not respond when they are over-taxed, they must be *coaxed*, and this is best achieved through a regular and progressive build-up of the resistance applied—plus, in some cases, adjustment to the number of repetitions, according to physical 'type'.

Slimmer types generally make quicker progress if they employ fairly high poundages with comparatively few repetitions. This type of training schedule, whilst fully activating the various muscle groups, is not exhaustive and the aim of the underweight man must always be to *conserve* energy. High repetitions would tend to wear him out, making him tougher and stronger, but not bulkier in size.

The hefty types, on the other hand, can cope with high repetitions *and* plenty of weight. They can, and must, employ comprehensive work-outs and it matters not if they burn up energy. It will help in the build-up of muscular size, with strength in proportion. The world's best-built men were not all 'naturals' to begin with. Some of the muscular giants started out with above average development, but as many were just ordinarily built lads when they took up bodybuilding, winning through to top honours via regular training on good progressive work-outs.

A glance at the 'Ideal Proportions Chart' will give some indication of the measurements you may ultimately achieve —but do *not* rely too much on the tape measure. It's what you *look* like that counts. Pay particular attention to good posture and at all costs avoid the 'tough guy' swagger when you walk. Nothing looks more ridiculous and will only bring you, and the sport of bodybuilding, into disrepute. Do try to be as natural as possible in the way you dress and conduct yourself generally. People will not have to be told about your fine physique. The well-built man always stands out in a crowd. You can be such a man.

Here is a training schedule for all-round muscular improvement for men of normal or average build:—

1. Press from Behind Neck (Page 82) 3 sets of 8 repetitions.
2. Seated, Single Arm Curl (Page 70) 3 sets of 8.
3. Upright Rowing (Page 84) 3 sets of 10.
4. Breathing Squat (Page 75) 3 sets of 12.
5. Pullover with Dumbells (Page 76) 3 sets of 10.
6. Bench Press with Barbell (Page 78) 3 sets of 10.
7. Single Arm Rowing (Page 106) 3 sets of 12 each arm.
8. Standing Heels Raise (Page 92) 4 sets of 15.
9. Sidebend with Dumbell (Page 99) 2 sets of 30 each side.

This training plan should be used three times weekly preferably in the evenings, at evenly spaced intervals. (Mondays, Wednesdays and Fridays are the popular training nights). Working hard, the full routine should take approximately one hour to perform, including rest periods between exercises—which should be of short duration.

Men of very light build will find the above schedule rather too exhausting and they will make much quicker progress by employing just 4 or 5 picked exercises, to encourage general muscle growth. Here is a good sample schedule, one that has proved highly successful with a large number of men of light skeletal structure:

1. Press from Behind Neck (Page 82) 4 sets of 6 repetitions.
2. Breathing Squat (Page 75) 4 sets of 8.
3. Bench Press with Barbell (Page 78) 4 sets of 6.
4. Barbell Rowing (Page 105) 3 sets of 8.
5. Dead Lift (Page 103) 4 sets of 5.

Note the relatively small number of repetitions—sufficient thoroughly to exercise all muscles concerned but not enough to over-tire or "burn-up" energy.

Now a word about weights: the *correct* poundage to use for each exercise. This is ascertained, in the first instance, by a little trial and error. What you must do is select a poundage that will just allow the full number of repetitions to be performed. If you discover that you are able to skip through all the repetitions of, say, the Dead Lift, easily, and without undue effort, then the weight is too light. The right poundage is one that will just, and *only* just enable you to complete all 4 sets of repetitions, whilst observing correct lifting style throughout. If you cannot manage the last few counts, then the weight must be reduced. It is not over difficult to select the proper starting poundages and you will soon become quite expert at knowing exactly what your capabilities are.

Remember, however, that your strength will increase very rapidly, which means you must add to your training poundages at regular intervals to ensure thorough and adequate working of the muscles. Normally one should increase the poundages used at every fourth work-out.

After ten weeks, it is time to alter the training schedule, and this you can easily do by changing each exercise for a similar one taken from the appropriate specialisation chapter. For example, the Press from Behind Neck could be changed for the Seated Dumbells Press—and so on. It is important, too, that you retain a pressing movement, Squat and Bench Press as the basic plan, as this is beneficial to all types and good for promoting all-round muscle growth.

On completion of your work-out, take a tepid shower (or sponge over with tepid water) followed by a brisk rub down with a coarse towel. This will set your skin a-tingle and give you that on-top-of-the-world feeling. Man, you'll feel great!